For Karl, with
Friendly wishes.
Fred

Out of My System

Out of My System

PSYCHOANALYSIS, IDEOLOGY,
AND CRITICAL METHOD

Frederick Crews

New York ₩ OXFORD UNIVERSITY PRESS ₩ 1975

Can Literature Be Psychoanalyzed? First published as "Literature and Psychology" in *Relations of Literary Study: Essays on Interdisciplinary Contributions*, edited by James Thorpe. Copyright © 1967 by the Modern Language Association of America.

Norman O. Brown: The World Dissolves. First published as "Love in the Western World" in *Partisan Review*. Copyright © 1967 by Frederick Crews.

Conrad's Uneasiness—and Ours. First published as "The Power of Darkness" in *Partisan Review*. Copyright © 1967 by Frederick Crews.

Anaesthetic Criticism. First appeared in *New York Review of Books*. Copyright © 1970 by Frederick Crews.

Student Protest and Academic Distance. First published as "The Radical Students" in *New York Review of Books*. Copyright © 1969 by Frederick Crews.

Do Literary Studies Have an Ideology? First published in *PMLA #85*. Copyright © 1970 by the Modern Language Association of America.

Offing Culture . . . First published in *TriQuarterly*. Copyright © 1972 by Frederick Crews.

Anxious Energetics. First published in *Partisan Review*. Copyright © 1974 by Frederick Crews.

Reductionism and Its Discontents. First published in *Critical Inquiry*. Copyright © 1975 by Frederick Crews.

For Betty, Gretchen, and Ingrid

ACKNOWLEDGMENTS

Chapters of this book were first published, with minor differences and in some cases under other titles, in *Partisan Review, PMLA, The New York Review of Books, TriQuarterly, Critical Inquiry,* and an MLA volume entitled *Relations of Literary Study: Essays on Interdisciplinary Contributions.* I am grateful to all the editors who granted permission for republication.

For generous support I am indebted to the American Council of Learned Societies, the John Simon Guggenheim Foundation, the Center for Advanced Study in the Behavioral Sciences, and the Regents of the University of California. First Whitney Blake, and then James Raimes, of Oxford University Press have patiently borne my delays and changes of intent.

My many drafts have been scrupulously edited, as ever, by Elizabeth Crews. Among others who have helped me with criticism, encouragement, or both, I would like to single out José Barchilon, Noam Chomsky, Norman N. Holland, Robert LeVine, Bernard C. Meyer, Ralph W. Rader, Murray M. Schwartz, Mark Shechner, Henry Nash Smith, and Ian P. Watt.

PREFACE

A reader casually looking through the essays in this book is bound to be puzzled by their apparent discontinuity. Psychoanalysis, to be sure, is to some degree involved in all of them, and four chapters deal directly with Freudian literary criticism: an introduction to that school, an example, a manifesto, and a warning against occupational hazards. But why, if the main concern is with applied analysis, should there also be discussions of lapsed and deviant Marxists, liberal warmakers, therapeutic utopians, and academic guerrillas? And why the tone of righteousness against positions that would never have tempted most people in the first place? That tone may sound especially odd to a reader who notices that in some respects these essays quarrel, not just with adversary views, but with one another. Shouldn't the author, instead of making us relive his intellectual and political vicissitudes, have arrived at a consistent stand and straightforwardly expounded it?

That was my intention when I conceived the earliest plan for this book a decade ago. But plans of every sort were ambushed by events in that decade. The Vietnam war, for one thing, didn't simply distract me from my psycholiterary investigations; it briefly turned me into a radical polemicist who had somehow to reconcile his academic with his oppositional instincts. That task was rendered harder for me by the student uprisings of the late sixties, which pitted some of my allies in the antiwar movement against fragile and irreplaceable institutions. The story of professorial ambivalence is familiar enough. In my case, however, the effort to work out a consistent attitude toward radicalism in its newest guises proved to bear directly on the methodological inquiries I kept postponing. Essays that were written as acts of political self-scrutiny, exploring why I felt uneasy about movements I might have been expected to applaud, also amounted to partial reappraisals of psychoanalysis as a "radical" doctrine. At last I realized that instead of being continually diverted from my book, I had nearly completed it. Its true subject, I discovered, was not psychoanalytic method per se, but the difficulty of mediating between empirical responsibility and urges toward deep and revolutionary explanation.

Discontent with my successive attempts to marry evidential circumspection and explanatory zeal has made this book an evolving document, an oblique case history of sorts. Rather than try to disguise that fact, I have emphasized it by printing the essays in order of composition, leaving them substantially unchanged, and adding headnotes that point to unsolved problems and shifts of attitude. But the "case" that thus emerges, I submit, is not just my own. Many people who don't share my interest in Freud have been temperamentally drawn toward interpretive schemes parallel in motive and habit to psychoanalysis in its most ambitious mood. They too face the pitfalls involved in asking a critical method to serve as a general philosophy. The impulse to make that leap—to stretch a skeptical technique of analysis into a sufficient conception of meaning and value—is what my book examines from various angles and finally rejects.

Purveyors of iconoclastic critical doctrines appear generally to be animated, not just by rational considerations, but by an intuitive anti-authoritarianism, a penchant for unearthing "real" significance that the established sages have been too timid or prudish or servile to acknowledge. Although this Oedipal fervor can easily get out of hand, in itself it seems no worse than many another motive that might be found to have influenced a scholar's work; it may even be a useful safeguard against pedantry. In certain circumstances, furthermore, an attempt to dismiss the whole prevailing framework of interpretation and to recast problems in "deep" terms may end by revitalizing a field in which taxonomic or configurational models have been carried to a point of diminishing returns. In linguistics, for example, I think of Noam Chomsky's bold contribution, which has surely owed something to a fierce personal resistance to authority. Or again, the fact that a student of history or politics wants to expose the hidden interests of seemingly benign officials doesn't necessarily make him a less rational analyst than someone who lacks that compulsion. Thus, at a time when liberals were content to speak blandly of "miscalculation" and "quagmire," angry radicals scrutinizing American conduct in Southeast Asia were able to put the miscalculations into a larger systemic context of neocolonialism. What matters isn't whether the analyst can achieve perfect disinterestedness, but whether he sees the situation clearly and isn't carried by his antagonistic sentiment into thinking in clichés.

Quite often, however, intellectual rebels don't escape this peril. The animus that enables them to look on ruling paradigms with total disbelief also takes them beyond empirical caution and into circular and dogmatic reasoning—even, sometimes, into a more genuine authoritarianism than the mild eclectic reign they are spurning. The anxieties attending isolation or self-exile from the main intellectual community are appeased by an insistence on the absolute rightness of one's own attitude, a maligning of dissenters, a reduction of newly encountered problems to the few determinants that have already been identified as explanatory, and a shallow and intolerant utopianism proposing a simple inversion of dominating and dominated elements. Not just individuals, but whole critical movements can fall into those habits as they move from demystification of particular deceits to vindictive visions of a new order—or to empty theatrics against the current one.

How these reflections bear on Freudianism may not be immediately clear. People who know psychoanalysis only as a rather tortuous bourgeois therapy, or who have skimmed Freud and noted his modest and scrupulous airs, may not perceive the extent to which he too licensed a spirit of dogmatically rebellious interpretation. In his writings vast presumption—a wish to expose all hypocrisy, unify all knowledge, assume a godlike distance from deluded mankind—is pitted against empirical and mundane loyalties that make such ambitions look unrealizable. The result is continual production of that most unrevolutionary effect, irony. Within the orthodox psychoanalytic tradition, shielded as it is by medical respectability and ego-psychological circumspection, it is difficult to grasp the naked daring of the original Freudian vision. To appreciate that daring we have to attend either to Freud's incredulous opponents or, better, to his utopian improvers such as Wilhelm Reich, Herbert Marcuse, and Norman O. Brown, all of whom claim with some justice that they are rescuing Freud's revolutionism from Freud the sardonic doctor.

Though the Freudian radicals caricature psychoanalysis, their caricature is assembled from real features of the doctrine: an extreme distrust of manifest ideas and altruistic aims, a championing of instinct against inhibition, a deterministic emphasis on a handful of hidden factors, an imperious merging of biological and mental categories, and a claim of special insight based on possession of a desublimating, counterdeceitful technique of interpretation. These are intellectual staples of revolutionism in most of its modern forms. Their prominence in Freudian thought may indicate that psychoanalysis is less a science than a world view asserting that what society has tried to bottle up is more significant than what it has left uncensored.

If this is so—if psychoanalysis is essentially an illusion-shattering movement which tends to overturn received values and affirm the primacy of the repressed—then someone hoping to use Freudian method for straightforward exegetical purposes may have some serious reassessing to do. He can distinguish, as I have done more than once below, between relatively "scientific" and relatively "ideological" strains of psychoanalytic thought, and he can resolve to keep his distance from the latter. He can go farther and insist that it is only the Freudian stance of self-correction and attentiveness to conflict, not an adherence to specific points of dogma, that he means to cultivate. But these efforts at intellectual sanitation are only halfway measures sparing a muddled position from fundamental review. For Freudian method invariably turns up traces of the themes that Freudian doctrine declares to lie at the roots of psychic life, and those themes typically subvert the intended or naïvely apparent meaning of a text or action and replace it with a demonic excavated content, akin to the interests laid bare by Marxian analysis. Of course a Freudian needn't ideologize that content in Reichian or Lawrentian style. But neither can he avoid placing an a priori stress on it, for his whole system obliges him to regard cultural objects as products of a dynamic contest. It is as if an anthropologist, stumbling across an unknown tribe, were immediately to begin assimilating its mores to the strenuous philosophy of Social Darwinism. He might or might not learn something that way, but in either case he would be making portentous prejudgments and excluding rival possibilities.

Doubts like these have gradually wrought a change of focus in my essays about method. After trying for several years to fit my cultural and political observations into a psychoanalytic framework, I have come to place less reliance on subtleties and escape clauses *within* psychoanalysis and have concentrated instead on the need for a wider outlook. Now I see, for example, that exclusive attention to conflict is itself an "ideological" choice, one dictated less by the self-evident nature of art works than by a wish to regard them in a certain tough-minded light. The results thus obtained may, in a given instance, be valid and important; but their validity cannot be established solely by recourse to Freudian premises, for psycho-analysis as a hermeneutics is too prone to question-begging. This is why my final chapters ascribe such importance to general criteria of rationality. Though I myself was first drawn to Freud by his promise of a Faustian key to knowledge, I find that my most binding loyalty is not to a particular system but to the empirical attitude—an attitude that psychoanalysis honors in spirit but only fitfully exemplifies. And the experience of the sixties has left me convinced that a refusal to have one's outlook bounded by a closed interpretive system is not just a necessary intellectual stand, but also a political one of extensive consequence for the defense of free institutions.

Readers shouldn't expect, however, that this book will chart the metamorphosis of a militant Freudian into a mild eclectic or of a radical incendiary into a liberal fuddy-duddy. I have been something of a radical fuddy-duddy from the outset. All my essays, for better or worse, are internal dialogues between rebellion and caution. Hence their gravitation toward issues posed by irrationalist fringe movements, and hence too their odd sternness, which is chiefly directed against facile enthusiasms I have barely managed to avoid. My vocation, it seems, is to be forever deciding that I would rather not be a fanatic of one sort or another.

Which is not to say that I ever arrive at an ideal of passive broad-mindedness, as if the whole purpose of intellectual life were to keep from being aroused. To cite the dangers attendant on a method is not to endorse the smug and vacuous idea that methods should be set aside altogether. More specifically, though I eventually insist on an inherent, ineradicable reductive tendency in psychoanalysis, I do so in order to clarify the basis on which Freudian statements can continue to bid for wide acceptance. To recognize, as my book does in its somewhat zigzag way, that psychoanalysis is a tool suited only for certain operations when certain kinds of problems have been identified, is not to dispense with Freud, but on the contrary to mark out a territory within which he remains indispensable.

Berkeley   F. C.
March 1975

CONTENTS

Out of My System

Chapter One

CAN LITERATURE BE PSYCHOANALYZED?

D0123221

In 1966, when my avowedly psychoanalytic book on Nathaniel Hawthorne, *The Sins of the Fathers,* appeared, I was asked by the Modern Language Association to contribute an essay on psychological criticism for an interdisciplinary volume, *Relations of Literary Study.* The piece I wrote makes scant allowance for psychologies other than orthodox Freudianism, and it now strikes me as too charitable toward the scientific claims of psychoanalysis. But as a brief primer on critical uses and abuses of Freud, it can serve to introduce several problems that will be raised in later chapters.

I must begin by explaining a drastic simplification of my topic. Despite the fact that psychoanalysis has weaker empirical credentials than the experimental schools that prevail in American universities,[1] "psychology" will here be contracted to mean psychoanalysis. There are several reasons for this, beyond a wish to avoid the spirit of meandering tourism. Psychoanalysis is the only psychology to have seriously altered our way of reading literature, and this alteration is little understood by the affected parties. To dwell at length on the possible literary implications of physiological psychology, of perception and cognition psychology, or of learning theory would be to say more than the psychologists themselves have been able to say. Even Gestalt psychology, which does promise enlightenment about the perception of artistic form, has told us virtually nothing about literature.[2] We must give our attention here to those who have claimed it.

The historical prominence of psychoanalysis in literary studies is readily understandable. Literature is written from and about motives, and psychoanalysis is the only thoroughgoing theory of motives that mankind has devised. The moment we perceive that works of art can express emotional conflict, or that they contain latent themes, or that their effect on us is largely subliminal, we have entered the realm of interest that is uniquely occupied by Freudianism and its offshoots. The psychoanalyst offers us, with a presumption we are likely to resent, a view of the writer's innermost preoccupations, a technique for exposing those preoccupations behind the defenses erected against them, and a dynamic explanation of how the literary work is received and judged. It is not merely that literature illustrates psychoanalytic ideas, as it does the ideas of other systems, but that the psychoanalyst alone undertakes to find motives for every rendered detail.

Needless to say, literary people have been anxious to debate the validity of such awesome claims. Much of the debate, however, has been acrimonious and irrelevant, thanks partly to the embarrassing subject matter of psychoanalysis and partly to professional rivalry. The traditional critic sees the analyst as an uninvited guest whose muddy boots will smudge the figure in the carpet; the analyst pities the critic his inhibitions and offers him sexual enlightenment free of charge. And both of them frequently speak of psychoanalysis as if it were contained in the personality and tastes of its founder, who still evokes obedience or hostility nearly three decades after his death. If we are to do any better here, it might be well to review the nature of Freud's interest in literature and make a sharp distinction between this interest and the independent possiblities of psychoanalysis in the hands of a literary critic.

We may say that literary people have taken offense at both the special presumptions and the special successes of Freud. Profoundly influenced though he was by Sophocles, Shakespeare, Dostoevsky, and Ibsen, Freud had little patience with what we like to call the integrity of the work of art. The work, in Philip Rieff's explanation, "is something to see through; it is presumably best explained by something other than—even contradicting—itself. Every work of art is to Freud a museum piece of the unconscious, an occasion to contemplate the unconscious frozen into one of its possible gestures." [3]

Thus Freud was interested not in art but in the latent meaning of art, and then only for illustrative purposes. Like dreams, myths, and fairy tales, works of art supplied useful evidence of the primordial and monotonous fantasies of mankind, and of the processes of condensation, displacement, and symbolism through which those fantasies are both expressed and disguised. Such an emphasis is insulting to the artist,

who *thought* he knew what he meant to say, and to the moral
or formal critic, who prefers to dwell on what Freud regards as
peripheral "manifest content" and "secondary revision." And
the insult is compounded by its success. We may assume that
if Freud had been wholly mistaken in his notion of buried
themes, he would long since have ceased to provoke defenders
of literary tradition into outbursts against "reductionism,"
"pan-sexualism," and "psychoanalyzing the dead."

Freud's challenge to the creator and the lover of literature is
not contained merely in his undermining of surface effects and
stated intentions. The artist, Freud tells us, has "an in-
troverted disposition and has not far to go to become neurotic.
He is one who is urged on by instinctual needs which are too
clamorous; he longs to attain to honour, power, riches, fame,
and the love of women; but he lacks the means of achieving
these gratifications. So . . . he turns away from reality and
transfers all his interest, and all his libido too, on to the creation of his wishes in the life of phantasy, from which the way
might readily lead to neurosis." [4] If, as an heir of the Romantic
movement, Freud sometimes credited art with visionary truth,
as a bourgeois, a scientist, and a utilitarian he suspected it of
unreality and evasion. [5]

Thus the literary critic is not altogether wrong in seeing
Freud as a disrespectful intruder. Yet to move from perceiving
this to denying the relevance of dynamic psychology to criticism is, to say the least, a hasty step. We are free to use
Freud's interpretive techniques without endorsing his compet-
itive and ambivalent remarks about artists. Post-Freudian psychoanalysis, furthermore, offers theoretical grounds for taking
the consciously "adaptive" aspect of literature more seriously
than Freud did, and Freud's own views lead us beyond the
static "museum piece" criticism he usually practiced. Tempting as it is to dispose of a complex and disturbing subject by
means of ad hominem ridicule, such a method of argument is
unworthy of scholars.

Everything hinges on whether psychoanalysis gives a true or sufficiently inclusive account of mental processes—a question that obviously cannot be settled here. Certainly it would be futile to cajole the reader who has decided that his own common sense is psychology enough. Yet most literary students, I feel, are of two minds about psychoanalysis; they may be impressed by its wide acceptance but reluctant to undertake an arduous and confusing course of reading. To justify this reluctance they vaguely entertain some of the many persisting grievances against psychoanalysis and psychoanalytic criticism. In order to put the matter on more rational grounds I propose to review the most common of these grievances and ask whether they do in fact warrant the theoretical neglect of a field which has already influenced our critical practice—often, to be sure, in a surreptitious or ignorantly popularized way. Before turning to literary applications I shall deal with prevalent objections to psychoanalysis as a body of knowledge:

1. Being unverified and unverifiable by experiment, psychoanalysis cannot be called a science at all. It is simply a technique of therapy, or a system of metaphors.

It is in the nature of all experiments that variables be kept to a minimum and that the path of inference from effect to cause be fairly direct. Any theory of complex and dynamic mental acts, and especially one that includes an idea of unconscious "overdetermination," must therefore remain largely unverified by experiment. Yet it is questionable whether this is a telling point against psychoanalysis. The psychological school which most insists on laboratory verification, namely behaviorism, has necessarily confined most of its researches to animals and to relatively simple problems of stimulus and response. The gain in verifiability is achieved at the cost of never approaching the complexity of uniquely human motives.

In any case it is incorrect to say that psychoanalysis remains wholly unverified. Certain of its aspects *have* been tested by experiment, and have withstood as much scrutiny as experiment could cast on them.[6] Despite some overpublicized defections, furthermore, the confirmation and refinement of Freud's discoveries have been proceeding in a fairly orderly way for many years; the essential concepts of psychoanalysis have been adequate to characterize the findings of innumerable independent workers. Corroboration of unconscious themes and processes is also offered by an abundance of materials external to the analytic experience: jokes and errors, primitive institutions and ritual, myths, and of course literature itself. For an unverified science psychoanalysis has had a remarkably profound effect on such apparently unrelated disciplines as anthropology, sociology, and educational theory. While the literary scholar is righteously declaring himself free of Freudian influence, his wife may be absorbing it in homeopathic doses from Dr. Spock.

The charge that psychoanalysis is metaphorical is true but easily misinterpreted. Such concepts as id, ego, and superego are not meant to describe physiological entities but spheres of interest that must be postulated to account for the observed fact that mental acts express compromised intentions.[7] Curiously enough, the most questionable part of psychoanalysis in the eyes of many post-Freudians is its least metaphorical, most biological side, namely the theory of instinctual psychic energy.[8] The strength of psychoanalysis may be said to lie in the precision of its metaphors—by which I mean their capacity for economically describing a vast range of evidence for which no other descriptive terms have been found. Where those metaphors need further refinement, as in the unwieldy overlapping of "topographic" and "structural" systems, the task will not be to adopt a more physical vocabulary but to achieve a parsimony of inferred concepts.[9]

2. *The layman has no basis for choosing among the many schismatic sects of psychoanalysis, and so should ignore them until they settle their differences.*

This would be sound advice if there were any likelihood that individual psychoanalysts, ambitious of glory, would stop founding new ideologies on isolated portions of theory. The student who cannot wait forever to decide what to think about human motivation must try as best he can to discriminate between such popular ideologies and genuinely empirical critiques of psychoanalysis (like those cited in footnotes 6, 8, and 9). If, for example, a rival system has had no medical consequences and has become a program of secular salvation rather than of therapy; if it has abandoned or attenuated the idea of dynamic conflict in favor of a monolithic and omnipresent explanation (trauma of birth, inferiority complex, collective unconscious, etc.); if it depends upon the support of religious and literary pieties and moral commonplaces divorced from clinical evidence—then, I think, suspicion is demanded. The literary student seems peculiarly vulnerable to pseudo-scientific improvements of psychoanalysis which dispense with sexual nastiness and glorify creativity. "Of the artist's relations to the psychologist," Edward Glover has written, "it can be said with some justice that their cordiality is in inverse ratio to their depth." [10]

This is not to say that one may fall back on Freudian orthodoxy as if it were revealed truth. Like all systems originating in a feeling for the indescribable, psychoanalysis has seen its metaphors reified, its hypotheses hardened into dogma, and its particular area of interest mistaken for total existence. Freud himself was not always above these tendencies, and few of his followers have shared his grasp of the difference between psychological reality and the conceptual framework needed for discussing that reality. Furthermore, on the positive side, present-day psychoanalysis has passed beyond Freud's almost exclusive emphasis on instinctual demands and infantile traumas to consider adaptive functions at all stages of development. The result remains "Freudian"—nearly all the principles of ego psychology are derived from hints in Freud's later writings—but not in the reductive sense that has most requently alienated non-Freudians. By reference to the so-called "conflict-free sphere of the ego," analysts now take better account of normal mental processes. Mastery of conflict is now as prominent as submission to conflict—a fact of moment for students of artistic creativity.

When this shift is considered along with Freud's own reformulations from decade to decade, the layman will feel properly discouraged from using any single text as his guide to psychoanalysis. If he intends to involve himself in the subject at all he had better be resigned to plodding through a certain amount of dreary polemics. Fortunately, however, clear explanations of the progress and quarrels of psychoanalysis are readily available and may be used to supplement a reading of one of Freud's sets of introductory lectures, which remain the most engaging means of initiation.[11]

I turn now to objections to the effect of psychoanalytic ideas and methods on literary criticism:

3. *The psychoanalytic view of the writer as a neurotic is presumptuous and condescending. Psychoanalysis is unequipped to describe the way writers really work.*

Even Freud was careful never to say that the artist is directly neurotic, and he admitted—perhaps hastily, many now feel—that psychoanalysis "can do nothing towards elucidating the nature of the artistic gift, nor can it explain the means by which the artist works—artistic technique." [12] Certainly Freud's disproportionate emphasis on unconscious factors had a pernicious effect on the first ventures into psychoanalytic criticism. Ludicrous diagnoses of writers' mental diseases, uninfluenced by historical or biographical knowledge or by literary taste, continue to appear regularly in the pages of clinical journals. Yet these efforts are more than bad criticism, they are bad psychology as well. It cannot be too strongly affirmed that psychoanalytic theory, especially in recent years, finds no necessary connection—at the most a useful analogy—between artistic production and the production of neurotic symptoms.

This analogy rests on the supposition that both art and neurosis originate in conflict and may be conceived as ways of managing it. But whereas the neurotic's solution is the helplessly regressive and primitive one of allowing repressed ideas to break into a disguised expression which is satisfying neither to the neurotic himself nor to others, the artist has the power to sublimate and neutralize conflict, to give it logical and social coherence through conscious elaboration, and to reach and communicate a sense of catharsis. The chief insistence on creative strength—on the artist's innate capacity for sublimation, his ability to handle dangerous psychic materials successfully—has come from within the psychoanalytic movement, not from outraged traditionalists. In truth, the theory that the artist is an especially morbid type antedates psychoanalysis and serves the very un-Freudian purpose of exaggerating the common man's freedom from conflict. It is thus a form of philistinism—one to which bad psychoanalysts have been susceptible but which is contrary to the whole spirit of the movement. "Of all mental systems," Lionel Trilling has justly written, "the Freudian psychology is the one which makes poetry indigenous to the very constitution of the mind. Indeed, the mind, as Freud sees it, is in the greater part of its tendency exactly a poetry-making organ." [13]

In a psychoanalytic view the artist is exceptionally able to make imaginative use of capacities which are present in everyone, but which are largely unavailable to expression in the noncreative man and are bound to self-destructive strife in the neurotic. The artist may, of course, be impelled by a certain degree of neurotic conflict to submit himself to unconscious dictates; this corresponds to the undeniable observation that great numbers of artists *are* neurotic. But neurosis alone cannot produce art and is inimical to the preconscious elaboration and the sublimation that make art possible. Insofar as he is neurotic, therefore, the artist is deficient in the functions that distinguish art from symptom formation. [14]

This is not to say, of course, that we are free after all to treat artistic creation and the aesthetic experience as special events in which the laws of mental dynamics are suspended. Many literary scholars are eager to believe those psychologists who, like C. G. Jung and his followers, sweep the element of personal conflict out of view and thus prepare the way for a mystic reverence for artistic truth.[15] But the literary work which is completely free from its biographical determinants is not to be found, and in many of the greatest works—the prime example is *Hamlet*—unresolved emotion and latent contradiction are irreducibly involved in the aesthetic effect. To appreciate why there are gaps in the surface we must be prepared to inspect what lies beneath them.

An aesthetic theory which ignores the possibility that latent and manifest content, unconscious and conscious purpose may be imperfectly harmonized is, to my mind, more reductive than a theory in which art represents a complex, "overdetermined" adjustment of varying psychic interests. One must decide whether to see art as a mental activity or as a direct apprehension of truth and beauty. The former attitude is less exalted, but it leaves the critic freer to trace the actual shape of a work, including its possible double meanings or confusions and its shifts of intensity and mood. The final word on the tiresome debate about art and neurosis should be that art need not express neurotic traits, but may very well do so in any individual case; the critic must wait and see.[16]

4. Psychoanalytic criticism neglects literary form, reduces all writers to an undifferentiated substratum of sexual obsession, and discards a writer's stated intention for a supposed unconscious one.

If this is taken as a description of much psychoanalytic criticism to date, rather than a statement of inherent limitations in the psychoanalytic attitude, then I must agree that it is accurate. Unfortunately, most literary people do not recognize this distinction; the "Freudian reductionist" is used as a scarecrow to protect the scholar's private harvest of literary history or factual detail or didactic moralism. It is true, of course, that a critical method which seizes upon a few unconscious themes and pronounces them the whole meaning of the work is grossly levelling; it is also true that Freud's technique of dream interpretation lends a certain inadvertent sanction to this approach. But the differences between dream and literature have long been recognized, as have the differences of purpose between the psychoanalyst, who is interested only in the mind that produced the dream or poem, and the critic, who must respect the object itself—including the elements in it which the analyst would regard merely as subterfuge. To say that psychoanalytic criticism *cannot* do justice to literary complexity is to suppose, as the worst psychoanalytic critics do, that an interest in psychological evidence can have no other purpose than to explain away manifest emphasis.

In shifting toward ego psychology, psychoanalytic theory has become better adapted to a study of the higher mental processes that enter into artistic creation, and to recognition of a communicative as well as a self-expressive function. It was a psychoanalyst, Ernst Kris, who insisted that the "reality" from which a literary creation proceeds is not only the reality of the author's drives and fantasies, but also the structure of his artistic problem and the historical state of his genre.[17] Indeed, nothing (other than inadequate acquaintance with tradition) prevents the psychoanalytic critic from considering exactly the same factors that concern the literary, the social, and the intellectual historian. As psychoanalysis has approached a point of reconciliation with social psychology, so too have psychoanalytic critics begun to turn their attention to broader matters than the unconscious fixations of a few unhappy writers. There have been numerous recent attempts to define the psychological quality of entire genres and movements, and even to take a psychological view of forces operating through history.[18] Nor has the psychology of form and style remained unexamined. Kenneth Burke—himself a Freudian of a maverick sort—once defined form as "an arousing and fulfillment of desires." [19] The idea has been pursued by several investigators, perhaps most successfully by Simon O. Lesser.[20] Form is being increasingly recognized not only as an aid to perception but as a vehicle of pleasure, including the pleasure of reducing the anxieties that other aspects of the work bring into play.

As for the author's stated intention, the subtlest modern critics have rightly placed little value on it—but not always for good reasons. The most celebrated dogma of the New Criticism has been that statements made before or after the literary fact must be considered less reliable than statements inferred from the text. All too often, however, this sound principle allows the critic to overstate the work's unity of effect or to drain off its passion and leave behind only a fragile tissue of symbols. By invoking the Intentional Fallacy the critic may fail to consider divisions of intention that are intrinsic to the work's structure and effect. I submit that we are entitled to consider *both* overt purpose and the perhaps contradictory purpose (or purposes) that may emerge from imagery or the shape of a plot. Psychoanalytic criticism has customarily occupied itself with the latter sort alone, but here too the historical reasons for this bias have lost their strength. In principle at least, the theory of overdetermination should enable us to feel more at home with literary tensions and contradictions than the critic who is searching only for leading ideas or unitary "meaning."

5. It is impossible to psychoanalyze dead writers, and anachronistic to apply Freudian rules to writers who lived before Freud.

Freud himself maintained the former truism, though he egregiously violated it in his study of Leonardo. There is a difference, however, between guessing at the infantile sources of trauma in an absent figure and identifying general psychological themes in a literary document. Freud's brilliant essay on Dostoevsky provides a model of the latter, more legitimate, kind of investigation.[21] To be sure, Freud draws on biographical materials and his own clinical knowledge to arrive at a speculation about the source of Dostoevsky's dominant theme; but our apprehension of Dostoevsky's literary qualities is richer for the speculation. An analysis of imagery or a repeated theme, when handled with discretion, can supply for the critic part of what the practicing analyst might gather more reliably from the patient's associations. It is a risky business, as countless pratfalls by psychoanalytic critics remind us. Most recent Freudians have acknowledged the dangers of biographical inference and have turned their attention to the structure of the literary work at hand, or to the varying responses it elicits from the reader.[22]

One may also detect a new caution about ascribing a psychological prehistory to literary characters—the most ridiculed of all Freudian practices. Much early psychoanalytic criticism, especially the efforts by physicians who were only dabbling in literature, perpetuated the quaint Victorian error of treating *homo fictus* as a completely knowable person. There is a qualitative gap between Mrs. Clarke's *Girlhood of Shakespeare's Heroines* and Ernest Jones's *Hamlet and Oedipus* (London, 1949), but they are connected by an embarrassing thread of tradition. Still, Jones is more faithful to the genuine puzzle of *Hamlet* than are the circumspect followers of E. E. Stoll, who solve essentially psychological problems by recourse to theatrical convention. What psychoanalytic criticism needs, in my opinion, is not an injunction against seeing arrested development in literary heroes, but a vocabulary for describing a work's implied psychological pattern without mistaking that pattern for the hero's case history. Hamlet may not have an Oedipus complex, but *Hamlet* does.

The charge of anachronism is easy to refute. It implies that at a certain moment Freud made human nature Freudian. To say that pre-Freudian men cannot illustrate psychoanalytic principles is simply to say that psychoanalysis is wrong—a

position which ought to be argued without recourse to the
sophistry of anachronism. Academic logic has never been
shakier than in recent efforts to prove that the psychological
insight of certain writers may be completely explained by the
mental theories current in their day. The reader must be dull
of soul who can be persuaded that Shakespeare is contained in
Timothy Bright, or that Hawthorne and Melville were disciples
of the sunny moralist Thomas C. Upham. Perhaps we need to
be reminded of Freud's own discovery that the essential features of his system were anticipated by poets and novelists—
or, more simply, perhaps we should have some faith in the literary imagination.

6. *Psychoanalytic criticism identifies unconscious content with literary value.*

Like other objections we have reviewed, this one is historically but not theoretically warranted. The psychoanalytic
movement has carried with it a fringe of zealots—we may
include in this category such otherwise diverse persons as the
Surrealist painters, D. H. Lawrence, Wilhelm Reich, and Norman O. Brown—who have preached a total escape from repression. This is not the goal of psychoanalysis, nor is it the
summum bonum of Freudian criticism. Freud's aim was not to
celebrate and release the unconscious but to bring its destructive tendency under rational control. While treasuring the evidence of unconscious processes in literature, he did not imagine that mere seizure by unconscious forces made a good
writer or a good work.[23] On the contrary, he complained of
Dostoevsky that "his insight was entirely restricted to the
workings of the abnormal psyche," and he showed how this
narrowness warped Dostoevsky's representation of love.[24]
Psychoanalytic critics have naturally been tempted to place
aesthetic value on what they have brought to light, and more
often than not it has been some compulsive pattern. But psychoanalytic theory clearly states that art depends on the ability

to manage and shape unconscious materials, not on those materials alone.[25]

7. *Psychoanalytic criticism is jargon-ridden.*

Here too we may grant the charge but deny that it will inevitably apply to subsequent efforts. For several reasons the temptation to write in technical jargon has been greater for psychoanalytic critics than for most others. They have been subject both to a pride in sounding scientific and to a despair of placating the inevitable academic reviewers who will decry all technical language not drawn from the humanistic sewing circle.[26] One detects a Thersites-like pleasure in the analysts' declaration that the heart of some beloved classic is rotten with polysyllabic fixations which the reader will not be able to find in his college dictionary. Such tendencies can of course be kept in check.

At the same time, it seems to me doubtful that psychoanalytic criticism can ever be, as one of its distinguished advocates would like, "rendered completely acceptable to the non-psychologically oriented scholars." [27] Beyond a certain point the disguise of one's premises amounts to abandonment of them. How, for example, can one substitute the term "conscience" for "superego" without blurring the irrationality —even the savagery—with which self-punishment is often inflicted in literary plots? How can one substitute "self" for "ego" without losing the often necessary sense of conflicting interests *within* a character's "self"? True jargon is technical language used imprecisely or unnecessarily. The real danger is not that the critic will have to resort to clinical terms (thereby offending those who would have rejected his argument anyway), but that he will allow his focus to stray from the literary work to the psychological system (thereby using the system as a club rather than a tool).

I would not want this essay to be taken as a plea for recruits to a militantly Freudian criticism. While psychoanalytic ideas have permeated our intellectual life, attempts at relating psychoanalysis to literature in a programmatic way have been handicapped by the need for cumbersome explanations of theory and for rapid passage from one example to the next.[28] Our most respected critics—I think offhand of I. A. Richards, Edmund Wilson, W. H. Auden, William Empson, Kenneth Burke, Alfred Kazin, Lionel Trilling—have neither ignored Freudianism nor made it a battle cry; they have absorbed it into their literary sense, along with other complementary approaches. I would urge, however, that such eclecticism be distinguished from indifference to theory. Something more than intellectual fashion is involved in the choice of psychological premises; the critic who disavows any taint of Freudianism usually ends by concocting his own psychology, a home brew of conscious "experience" and moral prejudice. What Allen Tate once said of philosophy must therefore be said of psychological theory as well: by pretending not to use it in literary studies we are using it badly.[29]

Chapter Two

NORMAN O. BROWN: THE WORLD DISSOLVES

This essay of 1967 originated in my anguish and frustration over the Vietnam war, my consequent attraction to global theories of historical explanation, and my contrary allegiance to empirical standards. The early and concluding paragraphs sound melodramatic to me now, but the appraisal of Brown—that he is less a psychoanalytic thinker than a would-be guru who has inverted Freud for his own religious purposes—has been reinforced by his subsequent writings. As for Herbert Marcuse, mentioned briefly here, he indeed became more "radical" than I found him in *Eros and Civilization* and *One-Dimensional Man;* his later career is touched on in Chapter Seven.

Americans tend to pride themselves on their eagerness to solve the world's problems. In agency reports and Sunday supplements one finds much benevolent discussion of the steps that should be taken against war, overpopulation, poverty, famine, plague, pollution, and so forth. The discussion has a businesslike air; first you find the means and then you do the job. Yet this progressive spirit is inadequate to explain our behavior in actual cases—to take one instance, our government's withholding grain from millions of starving Indians last year during some ruthless bargaining over the terms of "cooperation" imposed by an American fertilizer combine. To my mind the exploitative aspect of this behavior was less interesting than the fact that few Americans who read about it seemed to consider it bothersome—and those who read about it include, no doubt, some future authors of articles on the plight of India. The relevant question is not "What can we do about India?" but "Why is it so hard for us to understand our own feelings toward India?" Marxian terms take us part way toward an answer, but in the last analysis they are insufficiently radical. Indifference or hostility toward those who are poor and distant and colored is a psychological matter, one which involves not only our economic interest but also our shared fantasies and our available modes of expressing feeling.

Enthusiasts of the Vietnam war, for example, are fond of showing that our involvement cannot be properly explained in "selfish" terms; they then go on to make such fanciful remarks about treaty obligations and the championing of self-determination and democracy—remarks which have no basis in any known facts—that one must interpret them as unconscious hypocrisy. Evidently there are unacknowledgeable gratifications in the busywork of this particular war: eradicating villages, poisoning the crops of whole districts, dropping thousands of tons of explosives within map coordinates which ought by the laws of probability to contain some enemy soldiers, bulldozing miles of jungle that may have been "infested" with "gooks," etc. The military ineffectuality of most of these enterprises does not seem to be demoralizing; on the contrary, there is a note of uplift in reports of the sheer choreography of each logistically intricate "operation." A week-long undertaking which flattens the countryside but makes no contact with opposing troops is felt to be "the biggest operation of the war" and *ipso facto* worthwhile. To account for this patent lunacy one must ask in all seriousness how the observed action expresses our society's needs to standardize its environment, to exercise its technical skills cathartically, to excrete its most dangerous products without staying to observe the mess, and to "show its muscle" before potentially mocking bystanders. At the very least we should expect our political scientists not to confine the notion of mass irrationality to Nazi Germany, as they like to do. We need an Erik Erikson and a Norman Cohn to analyze the Hitler within ourselves, and beyond this we need a theory that will make allowance for the element of fantasy in social dealings generally. It is conceivable that our survival might depend on a willingness to abandon utilitarian models of strife and instead to isolate the syndrome of *homo economicus*, who grasps and hoards, sublimates and rationalizes, purifies himself and contaminates others, shrinks from strangers and finally attributes to them the implacable destructiveness of his own temperament.

In recent years only Herbert Marcuse and Norman O. Brown have dared to speculate at length about a future order that could be based on a new mental economy. On close inspection, however, Marcuse's commitment to psychoanalysis ap-

pears far from revolutionary. The unfettering of instinct he
rather circumspectly entertains in *Eros and Civilization* entails
no rupture with the status quo. It would be "predicated not
upon the arrest, but upon the liberation, of progress"; it could
only be attempted "*after* culture had done its work and created
the mankind and the world that could be free." With this accommodation to the institutions he criticizes, it is little
wonder that Marcuse arrives at a wistful sentimentalism, offering little more than a vague prospect that death "can be made
rational—painless." [1] Again, in *One-Dimensional Man* Marcuse
locates his hope in "the completion of the technological reality," which would be "not only the prerequisite, but also the
rationale for *transcending* the technological reality." [2] This may
be good dialectics but it amounts to fatalism; Marcuse cannot
think beyond the welfare state and the self–improving hobbies
of leisure time. Brown, in contrast, promises nothing less than
a "diagnosis of the universal neurosis of mankind, in which
psychoanalysis is itself a symptom and a stage" [3]; and his
diagnosis is followed by a prescription for total cure.

To come under the spell of *Life Against Death*, as many of us
did eight years ago, is to be lifted suddenly above the plane of
academic cliché and to conceive a new intensity of self-inves-
tigation. Here, perhaps—and many readers still think so—was
a scientific refutation of all social ideals that negate the life of
the body. Perhaps psychoanalysis alone would suffice to decipher and redeem the irrationality of history. Though one could
do worse than to pursue this hope to the end, Brown as its advocate comes to seem less and less reliable as one's concern
shifts from personal catharsis to the misfortunes of classes and
states. One such disillusionment, at any rate, lies behind this
essay. My purpose in treating Brown at length is to show that
his use of psychological theory is finally a disservice to the important cause of applied psychoanalysis. I think it is necessary
to challenge the flourishing cult of Brown among scientifically
impressionable humanists—those who are drawn to any set of

ideas that defends poetic insight against factual positivism. When the ideas are as theoretically and empirically defective as Brown's, literary intellectuals who champion them merely reinforce their own role as innocuous traditionalists within a society that needs criticism, while psychoanalysis as a vital style of thought continues to languish in disrepute among the rest of the intellectual community.

Readers who know Brown's second ambitious book, *Love's Body*, with its elfin manner, its religious imagery, and its cryptic emphasis on self-immolation and a final silence, will not need to be told that he no longer seriously proposes to expound a scientific point of view. My impression, however, is that many of these readers dismiss the new book as "absolutely mad" and return to *Life Against Death* with undiminished faith in its claim to embody the Freudian outlook on history. But there is nothing mad about *Love's Body*; it has a strong internal logic, and its starting point is the philosophy of body consciousness that was already spelled out in the final chapter of *Life Against Death*. To be sure, Brown has been spiritually on the move, but he is no less trustworthy an authority on psychoanalysis than before. For the truth is that despite Lionel Trilling's encomium on *Life Against Death* as "the best interpretation of Freud I know," Brown has always been a blithely misleading guide through the thickets of factionalism, conceptual redundancy, and biological archaism that await every student of psychoanalysis. *Love's Body* may indeed be the more acceptable of the two books; because it insists on the nonliteral status of its propositions, it creates less misunderstanding about mental theory than *Life Against Death*.

In one substantial respect, however, Brown is a valuable commentator on psychoanalysis. Anyone who wants to use Freudian concepts to pose sweeping questions about mankind must face some ethical ambiguities within Freud's thought. This Brown has brilliantly done. He shows that the latent tendency of Freud's science cannot be bounded by Freud's personal stoicism and conservatism, his sardonic acquiescence in available norms; and he justly accuses many of Freud's successors of having betrayed the best psychoanalytic insight, namely that which would have discredited their peddling of culture-bound moral commonplaces under the label of objective knowledge. Psychoanalysis, as Brown shows with relentless polemical vigor, has never been able to decide whether it aims at individual therapy—i.e., conformity to the versions of tolerable unhappiness offered by a sick society—or at a social transformation that would weaken the antagonism between instinct and "reality." The confusion is not merely ethical; it extends deep into the theory itself. In its positivist mood psychoanalysis tells us that cure lies in rational mastery of what was formerly repressed: "where id was, there shall ego be." In its tragic mood it implies that sacrifices of instinct will be avenged by a resurgence from below; the most exacting sublimations will trigger the most catastrophic counterassaults by the repressed. Most importantly, Brown sees that in trying to pass muster among the quantifying, direct-observation sciences, psychoanalysis is disloyal to its own revolutionary perspective on knowledge. To a philosophical mind the chief merit of psychoanalysis is that it points a way out of the sterile Western categories of subject and object, inner and outer reality, thought and feeling, high and low motives. To have defended this possibility in the face of revisionist theory and conformist therapy is no small achievement.

Of course Brown promises much more than this. Witness the subtitle of the book he is known by: *The Psychoanalytical Meaning of History*. To follow Brown all the way is to "see history, as neurosis, pressing restlessly and unconsciously toward the abolition of history" (*LD*, p. 91), unless its course can be diverted into a general regression to the body erotism that supposedly antedates the oral, anal, and genital "organizations of the libido." I wish I could formulate this idea more clearly and still remain faithful to Brown's words; he seems quite earnestly to imply that history is to be redeemed by taking his advice. This, as Henry James said of Whitman's effort to identify himself with the third person of the Trinity, is tolerably egotistical. But merely to list the main steps Brown's claim requires us to make is to reduce it to absurdity. We must first agree that history can be usefully personified as a psychoanalytic patient, and we must not pause over such trifles as whether Eastern history is to be counted, whether history's case history forms a continuum across cultures and epochs, and whether there is any meaningful sense in which history can be regarded as harboring repressed memories of its infantile traumas. There is no sign that these questions have crossed Brown's mind. Next, having wrestled history onto the couch, we must assume that it will be found as sick as the sickest neurotic, heading for psychosis—for Brown sides with those who deny the possibility of successful sublimation. If history sublimates, squandering its libido on would-be refinements, then history is in for a vendetta from below. And we must also believe that significant numbers of men, including the main decision-makers of the world, will find themselves capable of consciously banishing repression from their lives. This may be the trickiest step of all, for we must assent to the most inexorably pessimistic Freudian argument about man's unconscious slavery and then declare that man is free to make himself over as he pleases.

It is unsettling to realize that Brown has not only failed to allay these doubts, but has not bothered to defend his generalities through illustration. If history is a deteriorating neurosis, we would like to see how one of its phases shows a greater domination by pathological factors than another. It is true that Brown characterizes early Protestantism as "a new stage in history, a fuller return of the repressed" (*LD*, p. 232); but fuller than what? Without any comparative discussion of the Catholic Middle Ages he can hardly be said to have scored a point. Indeed, his lively chapter on Luther's anality, the Devil, Prot-

estantism, and capitalism makes a case *against* his thesis, for
he repeatedly complains that modern Protestants have lost the
diabolism and eschatology that Luther once brought to the
surface. He does not disguise his irritation with an epoch
which is so little tormented by its unconscious conflicts that it
cannot appreciate the need for a (Brownian) kingdom of grace,
but he fails to notice that such an epoch falls outside his alleged dynamic of history. At the very least he might be expected to offer a crude sketch of "the repressed's" inroads between Luther's century and ours, but this too is missing.

My immediate concern is to show, not that Brown's alarmism
is unwarranted (maybe it isn't), but that his treatment of psychoanalysis is governed by the special requirements of his
argument. The result is a subtle perversion of the whole body
of Freudian theory. If that theory is germane to anything, it is
to the data unearthed in clinical experience, and any adjust-
ments in the theory are obviously to be judged on their capacity to account for the data more fully or more economically. To
Brown, however, psychoanalysis is a set of paradoxical propositions about human fate—propositions which only need a
little editing to be brought into alignment with his favorite
tradition of mystical and dialectical thought. In a word, psychoanalysis for Brown is not science but poetic philosophy,
just as its harshest critics have always said. Only on this assumption can we explain, for example, how he feels entitled to
assert with breathtaking audacity that Freud was wrong to
regard the sexual organizations as biologically determined.
The real meaning of such a statement is that Brown has come
across an obstacle to his utopianism and is wishing it away.

Much of Brown's trenchant prose looks devious in a critical
rereading. His strategy in general is to imply that Freud's
deepest insights can be preserved only in his own idiosyncratic and ideological formulations, which are offered as mere
clarifications of the master's ambiguities. What we tend to
recall from *Life Against Death* are Brown's telling jibes at intel-

lectual timidity: the timidity of those who blind themselves to
the bodily reference of symbolism, of those who shy away
from Freud's instinct theory because it leads to despair, of
those rival utopians who glorify one organ at the expense of
the whole body, of those modern Aeolists and breech-peepers
who must either call Swift mad or deny his anal obsession altogether, and thus "domesticate and housebreak this tiger of
English literature" (*LD*, p. 180). Brown is a virtuoso of cold
dismissal. He begins to seem fatally vague only when we ask
exactly how this analytic, Apollonian intellect of his can be
abrogated in favor of polymorphous perversity. After several
hundred pages the suspicion arises that Brown does not know
what he means by the undoing of repression or the mystical
body of childhood. At most we are left with a promise ("the
task of judicious appraisal . . . comes later"—*LD*, p. xi) which
Love's Body no longer pretends to postpone, much less to
honor.

Brown's handling of psychoanalytic terminology is cavalier
in the extreme. He is inevitably drawn to the most dramatic—
one is inclined to say melodramatic—aspect of Freudianism,
the Eros-Death dualism. Freud embarrassed most of his followers by taking this dubious hunch about the properties of
organic matter and using it to explain mental acts, but Freud at
least recalled occasionally that this was speculation, a philosophical overlay on the observables of psychoanalysis. Brown
in contrast is satisfied that a view of all life as composed of unstable fusions of Eros and Death will give maximum exercise
to the spirit of paradox. In this controversy as in others, he
never once deviates into petty considerations of evidence. Re-
sidual doubts are swept away with the clinching thought that
all the wrong people, the anti-Freudians and the plodding
therapists, reject instinctual dualism; the only reason it is
omitted from psychoanalytic orthodoxy must be that it is conducive to gloom. For Brown this gloom is something to be cul-
tivated and then dialectically overcome; by supposing that Life

and Death coexist in undifferentiated unity at the animal level one can pass to the millenarian hope that "they could be reunified into some higher harmony in man" (*LD*, p. 87). To recognize that psychoanalysis is chiefly a theory of psychic drives, structures, and compromises, not a theory about the contest between two bodily energies, would be to ring the curtain on Brown's cosmic melodrama.

Brown can be relied on to celebrate those points of theory that could be turned against Freud's ideal of adult normality—*"lieben und arbeiten,"* as he once put it with his genius for brevity. Brown's rhetorical task is to reduce *lieben* to body narcissism and *arbeiten* to sheer sickness. In order to do so he must resuscitate everything in Freudian thought that has proved least acceptable to physical scientists. Thus he embraces the biologically discredited idea that organisms are constantly dedicated to tension reduction, and he willingly follows Freud into intricate applications of the Nirvana principle to the human mind; "ageless religious aspirations" look quite up to date in such terms. Similarly, he is only too eager to accept Freud's hydraulic idea of "stores" and "reservoirs" of sexual energy that are set to one side by the classic traumas of childhood. Such a conception can be invoked at the proper moment to belittle the possibility of nonrepressive sublimation and to accuse the sexual organizations of being needlessly parsimonious with life. Only in this perspective can Brown say that psychoanalysis regards sociability itself as a sickness—a remark which is in fact nothing more than an article of Rousseauistic ideology on Brown's part. Above all, he clings to Freud's proposals that thinking is merely a detour to a remembered (infantile) image and that only the earliest wishes yield true gratification.

Brown's ferocity toward ego psychology, with its allowance for desexualized, autonomous, adaptive functions, is a necessary corollary of this stance, as is his admiration for the most zealous and speculative of id psychologists, Sándor Ferenczi and Géza Róheim. A Lamarckian *jeu d'esprit* like Ferenczi's *Thalassa*, which biologists disregard for excellent reasons, strikes Brown as a masterpiece because it dares to psychoanalyze all living matter throughout evolutionary time, and does so in terms of the Eros-Death theory. Brown and Ferenczi alike undertake the dubious task of applying a single set of terms to the amoeba and the ego, but Ferenczi at least confesses that he is thinking in analogies. With Ferenczi and Róheim, Brown has a taste for direct and deflating reductions of "advanced" capacities to the emotional crises that may have prompted their first use in a typical life history. The effect of such originology, as Erikson calls it, is to extend the concept of trauma across the whole domain of innate competence, as if man's unique gifts were somehow explainable as improvisations in the face of infantile disappointment. All language, says Brown, is made out of sexuality, and all thinking comes from anal erotism—that is, from perversion of Eros. "Since money breeds, the genital region is involved" (*LD*, p. 288) in the money complex. Social organization is merely (*à la* Róheim) a collective confession of guilt. The time sense is the work of repression and nothing more. Sublimations, such as music and mathematics, are negated instincts entering consciousness under false colors. Thus Brown sweeps out of view everything but an arbitrarily simplified "natural tendency of the human body" (*LD*, p. 110) and the deepest unconscious, which is now taken to be "the 'noumenal' reality of ourselves" (*LD*, p. 94). This inverted Transcendentalism is not the outcome of Brown's study of Freud but rather the governing theology behind that study.

We should therefore not be too surprised, when we turn to *Love's Body*, to find that Brown has abandoned propositional argument for visionary sayings—sayings which aspire to profundity yet also to childlike freedom from literal-minded intellectualism. "Wisdom is in wit, in fooling, most excellent fooling; in play, and not in heavy puritanical seriousness. In

levity, not gravity. My yoke is easy, my burden is light." [4]
Throughout *Love's Body* Brown is playing with words: punning, chasing true and false etymologies, self-consciously relax-
ing his rational guard. The phrases that get themselves uttered
are full of surprises ("a king is an erection of the body politic"—*L'sB*, p. 133) and no less full of preciosity: "the shell-
fishness of selfishness" (*L'sB*, p. 44). Any reader of *Love's Body*
will find sentences that strike him as sharply true and others
that seem not to go beyond the late A. A. Brill's notorious
view of poetry as a chewing and sucking of beautiful words.
Like Emerson—and those who have read Brown's Columbia
Phi Beta Kappa address of 1960, "Apocalypse," will remember
that the identification with Emerson is deep and acknowledged—Brown now disdains transitional logic in favor of
quotable, detachable sentences. [5] As reviewers have noted, the
influence of Marshall McLuhan is also prominent; like McLuhan, Brown seems to waver between scholarship and show-
manship. The orphic tone, the pregnant silences, the pompous
footnotes, the "empty words, corresponding to the void in
things" (*L'sB*, p. 259)—all have an onstage air. Bravely, Brown
has tried to redeem the latent promise of *Life Against Death*
and offer us polymorphous perversity epitomized in prose.
However successful one may judge the effort to be, it remains
an effort, a strained performance.

Brown has not altogether abandoned the rational façade of
his body mysticism. One can even detect a tacit shifting from
less defensible to more defensible ground, specifically from
late-Freudian instinct theory to Kleinian fantasy theory. Melanie Klein's ideas about the early months of infancy are, of
course, widely mistrusted, and evidence to confirm or discon-
firm them is hard to come by; but they have a whole school of
child analysis behind them, and in general they pose less of an
outrage to scientific respectability than do Eros and Thanatos,
which Brown now scarcely mentions. This is not to say,
though, that he has become an empiricist. The work most

frequently cited remains Ferenczi's *Thalassa*, which Brown still pretends to regard as a textbook of evolution; and he has by no means forsworn his habit of making a scrapbook of all psychoanalytic utterances that sound corroborative of his philosophy. The recourse to Kleinianism may be understood as an ingenious new attack on the reality principle. Just as Ferenczi shrank all genitality to the pathetic "dream of uterine regression," so Melanie Klein—adopting Ferenczi's own terminology, by the way—purported to show that dealings with "reality" are determined by fantasies, specifically by the introjection of parental figures. "Sadistic fantasies directed against the inside of [the mother's] body constitute the first and basic relation to the outside world and to reality." Thus Klein; and hence Brown: "the world is the insides of mother" (*L'sB*, p. 36).

Since remarks of this sort will sound imbecilic to most readers, I want to point out that Brown values them in part for heuristic or purgative reasons. Being opposed to the idea of separate selfhood, he declares that we have fashioned our egos solely by ingesting what is past and other; the boundary between inner and outer reality is artificial, a rampart of the repressive personality. Insofar as he is undermining the common prejudice, shared in much Freudian thought, that the realm of fantasy is less real than the impinging environmental demands, Brown is making a strong point. As he puts it, "Psychoanalysis began as a further advance of civilized (scientific) objectivity; to expose remnants of primitive participation, to eliminate them; studying the world of dreams, of primitive magic, of madness, but not participating in dreams or magic, or madness. But the outcome of psychoanalysis is the discovery that magic and madness are everywhere, and dreams is what we are made of" (*L'sB*, p. 254). We can recognize the hyperbole in such a statement and still find it intellectually liberating. Brown's invocation of Melanie Klein, like his use of Róheim and Ferenczi, is a refreshing means of being

more Freudian than Freud; it does give us a peculiarly sharp
view of Freud's ontological ambiguity and of the inadequacy
of his therapeutic ethic to contain his insight into the persistence of unconscious fantasy in every phase of life.

The usual unanswerable questions arise when we try to
move from Brown's attack on selfhood to his idea of salvation.
Here Melanie Klein's lurid picture of the fantasy-ridden
human suckling becomes an encumbrance, for exactly the reason that Freud's instinct theory was finally an encumbrance in
Life Against Death; to the degree that the theory depicts mankind as subject to routine infantile traumas, it makes the
Brownian utopia unbelievable. Having chosen to read psychoanalysis as tragedy, Brown finds himself obliged to rewrite the
script to allow for a redemptive "conscious magic, or conscious madness" (*L'sB,* p. 254). But once we have registered
the Kleinian vision of everything human as governed by unconscious projections and introjections, mostly of a murderous
nature, we can no longer conceive of the polymorphously narcissistic body of childhood. Brown's own sources expose the
emptiness of his cry, "Down with defense mechanisms,
character-armor; disarmament" (*L'sB,* p. 149).

In various tacit ways Brown now acknowledges the discontinuity between his values and their supposed evidential un-
derpinnings. He is much vaguer than before in alluding to the
end of history; no sustained analysis of movements or art
works is provided to match the fascinating chapters on Luther
and Swift in *Life Against Death;* no longer does he systematically attack the commonsense psychological assumptions
behind the social sciences. Indeed, he is no longer much concerned about the limits of acceptable psychoanalytic thought.
Whereas he once sneered at "Jungian *Schwärmerei*" and quite
properly characterized Jung's orientation as "flight from the
problem of the body" (*LD,* pp. 126, 313), now he uses words
like "soul" and "archetype" with literary abandon, and alludes favorably to the Jungian mythographers Kerényi and

Neumann. Perhaps a close reader of *Life Against Death* might have predicted this change, which is not so great if we realize that Brown's intent has been religious from the start; witness his incautious celebration of Mircea Eliade, to say nothing of Boehme and Berdyaev. It should also be mentioned that Brown's most radical pronouncements ("Work is a masturbation dream"; "All movement is phallic") are now delivered with a subdued, unpolemical air. The entire book seems almost to excuse itself as a verbal game, a self-conscious overvaluation of words. But I do not mean to say that Brown is insincere; the point is that he seems to recognize the privacy of his reflections and is content to have us keep our intellectual distance.

It is instructive to take up a psychoanalytic perspective on the most alarming aspect of *Love's Body,* its solemn and pervasive Christian language. Brown's crypto-religious declaration of independence from the Oedipus dilemma is highly suspect—is, indeed, virtually a filial confession. He rejects genital intercourse for the explicit reason that it constitutes a fantasied incest, and he identifies himself with Christ because, in his understanding, Christ is "a Son of God who is without a father . . . the Oedipus Complex transcended" (*L'sB,* p. 54). Freud would surely have smiled at the quaint idea of erasing the Oedipus Complex by pretending to be parentless; what is it but a variant of the family romance? And Freud would not have been startled to find this self-castrating advocate of pregenitality going on to revel in the sacrificial imagery of the cross. Much that seems bizarre in *Love's Body* makes sense in this way. If, as John Wisdom fairly well proved, Bishop Berkeley's Idealism involved an equation of matter with excrement,[6] Norman O. Brown's wished-for "crucifixion of the self" appears to be a quixotic anti-Oedipal maneuver. "There is no way to avoid murder," he says, "except by ritual murder" (*L'sB,* p. 172). Such sentences form a revealing gloss on the lyricism of polymorphous perversity; on the one hand they indicate why Brown *must* pastoralize a pre-Oedipal state; on the other hand they cast further doubt, if more is needed, on the supposed triumph over repression. A man who must comfort himself with the fantasy of being consumed in the Eucharist has not yet reentered the paradise of infancy. Is he nearer to it than *l'homme moyen sensuel?* One's mind returns to one of the earliest and most curious sentences in *Life Against Death:* "To experience Freud is to partake a second time of the forbidden fruit; and this book cannot without sinning communicate that experience to the reader" (*LD*, pp. xi–xii). Brown's spiritual career begins to look like a passage from such sinning to ritual atonement: from rebellious Luther to annihilated Christ.

It is Brown, of course, who has most eloquently warned us against the self-righteous use of psychoanalysis as a means of concealing our own irrationality; like Swift, he invites condescension because he deals openly with, and finally fails to resolve, conflicts which the psychological cowardice of mankind would prefer to keep disguised. Again, it is Brown who has shown us the narrowness of Freud's dismissal of religion as mere wishful thinking, to be replaced by rational science. Religion and psychoanalysis both are ways of coping with the madness that threatens every human generation, and each way is affected by what it opposes. As Freud confessed, "No one who, like me, conjures up the most evil of those half-tamed demons that inhabit the human breast, and seeks to wrestle with them, can expect to come through the struggle unscathed." [7] We may prefer psychoanalysis to religion on both intellectual and medical grounds, yet still recognize that it is unreasonable to demand of any thinker—even a psychoanalytic one—that he purge himself of theological nuances. Regardless, therefore, of the personal determinants behind Brown's eccentric form of Christianity, we might profitably ask what his books reflect about the culture we share with him.

In the broadest and simplest view we might say that Brown's appeal rests on his anti-intellectualism; perhaps no one has ever marshalled such a show of learning in behalf of an end to rational knowledge. The contradictions and non sequiturs in his argument seem unimportant to many readers, so anxious are they to believe what Brown is telling them. As men begin to articulate their feeling of slavery to the tools and the inorganic surroundings they cannot stop creating, reason itself is chosen as their scapegoat. Dispassionately considered, Brown's works ought not to strengthen this prejudice; one of his cardinal points, after all, is that unreason lies at the base of our money and production systems. Heinz Hartmann wrote in 1937 that no society has ever labored under a surfeit of intelligence; the point remains true. But in fact Brown is as anxious as anyone to indict reason along with the compulsions that act in reason's name. If few of his adherents show any skepticism toward "The Psychoanalytical Meaning of History," it is not because his vacant laws of recurrence are pondered and believed, but on the contrary because he insinuates that we needn't believe in history at all. As Hayden V. White has recently argued, *Life Against Death* is antihistory, a downgrading of the whole idea of bothering about the past.[8] In this sense it matches the antagonism toward impersonal, chronological history shown by virtually every significant modern writer. White finds this antagonism refreshing because it opposes stale conventions of history writing, but surely this is trivial next to the shattering thought that the Western world may be losing faith in the meaningfulness of its past. The vogue of Norman O. Brown appears to coincide with a suspicion among many literate people that man's cultural ideals have always been illusory, and hence that the accumulated bloodshed of history has been a farcical waste.

This suspicion is understandable, but it is less clear why Brown's humorless utopianism should seem different in kind from the vanities of the past. The utopias that Marx ridiculed and the one he finally advocated were less of an affront to the best knowledge of their time than is Brown's reign of body narcissism. But Brown's appeal is precisely to those whose one intellectual conviction is that they have been bypassed or slandered by "knowledge." Sick of ideology, unsatisfied by notions of impersonal and objective truth, violated in their selfhood by McLuhan's omnipresent electronic nervous system, many are ready to believe that social existence itself is a swindle. They are ready to toy with a new religion, but only a religion of solipsism which confines its message to a promise of perfect self-indulgence.

Here Philip Rieff's brilliant study, *The Triumph of the Therapeutic,* seems to offer the right framework for comprehending Brown's career. Western intellectuals, he says, are staging an elaborate act of suicide, an apostasy from the cause of culture to the primitive forces that culture is supposed to master. Rieff shows that unlike Freud, who saw no alternative to social restraints and was superbly reconciled to the pettiness of human fate, certain influential moderns have turned psychoanalysis to the purposes of ultimate cure—a cure for individuals that disregards or even dispenses with society as a whole. The choice of psychoanalysis seems natural in view of Rieff's formula: "faiths develop first as primary modes of release from earlier uses of faith, and then develop their own control functions." [9] Whatever its merit as science, psychoanalysis has served as a mode of release from faith—indeed, as potentially the most anarchic release in history, since it undermines not only specific taboos but the very category of the sacred. It is to be expected that some thinkers who have lived for a while with this unnerving perspective will cast about for new certainties in the realm of instinct, and will pose these certainties in psychoanalytic language. Hence Jung, Wilhelm Reich, and Lawrence, among others, celebrate the natural man and use Freudian terms to rail against the sober pessimism of Freud. Each sets his sights on redemption; each corrupts the dynamic and descriptive scheme of psychoanalysis into monism and moralism. The lost soul of modern man may yet be recovered—in

orgasm, in orgone energy, in the tasteful museum of unconscious archetypes. In each case the element of social control is
minimal, as befits an age demanding what Rieff calls remissive
blasphemy, in contrast to the repressive piety of the past.

Norman O. Brown's case should form a revealing appendix
to Rieff's analysis, for Brown is at once more reductive and
more remissive than his fellow prophets. Instead of the sac-
charine eclecticism of Jung, who somehow managed to imply
that instinct and culture were not opposed after all, Brown
purports to abolish every trace of sublimation. His world is
peopled exclusively by penises and vaginas; but since for him
these are items of symbolism—since the sex act itself is symbolic, and nothing is real but imagination—it follows that man
is totally unconstrained at last. The dionysian Christ requires
nothing of us, not even assent to his existence. Again, if we
consider the political dimension of *Love's Body* we can see that
Brown has trumped his predecessors. Reich was a Marxist,
Lawrence had a streak of latent fascism, and Jung welcomed
Hitler in Wagnerian tones. Brown outdoes them all in one sentence: "The real prayer," he says, "is to see this world go up
in flames" (*L's B*, p. 177). But then he reminds us that literal
interpretations are vulgar; by making his fantasy explicit, by
allowing the repressed to return uncensored, he has made it
innocent of covert violence. A man who rejects hierarchy in
human faculties will be against dictatorship on all levels. Polymorphous perversity seems indeed to be the acme of quietism;
it requires no partner, overburdens no organ, and entails no
direct social consequence. One might add that it entails no
discipleship to Norman O. Brown. Insofar as he has succeeded
in keeping his body mysticism uncluttered by Jung's cultural
trappings or the social criticism of Reich and Lawrence, he has
disencumbered himself of followers who might have seen him
as the champion of their grievances. In the decade of self-
destroying sculpture Brown has perfected a new form, the self-
abolishing movement.

With *Love's Body* Brown abandons his questionable role as historian and gives himself over to the ingenious nihilism that was lodged between the lines of *Life Against Death*. He eliminates our problems by eliminating us. Therapeutic Idealism, which has been out of favor with most intellectuals at least since the time of Mrs. Eddy, here undergoes another birth in the guise of its opposite, total desublimation. Set free from all neurotic striving, Eros politely agrees not to be a nuisance any more and retires to the domain of symbolism. Nothing remains for us to do but pluck our insipid lutes within a Oneness which is now devoid of content. The distant explosions we thought we heard—they too must be interpreted according to the spirit. And if the bombs should turn out to be real after all, and begin falling on us, they will find us in a serene attitude: passive, pre-Oedipal, androgynous.

The business of philosophy, of course, is not to make protest but to explore the nature of reality and language, and to alter or refresh our sense of what is important. Brown is not to be blamed for seeming indifferent to napalm and hydrogen bombs and planned epidemics; perhaps we *should* be indifferent to them, i.e., immune to their sadistic appeal. It is worth recalling that a Herman Kahn speaks "realistically" of such things yet remains their obedient slave. The war machine is not likely to be stopped by those who are obliged to think in the war machine's language. Brown at least sets up rival terms of discourse and reminds us vividly of the unconscious life that is stepped on and twisted but never quite killed by the aggressive technological mentality now reigning. He goes wrong where all primitivism does, in making a static idol of the buried life, and so turning what might have been a dynamic analysis into an ideological allegory. Instead of abolishing history for the rest of us—indeed, instead of making historical statements that are sufficiently complex to warrant trust—Brown seems headed for the ironic fate of becoming himself an episode in the history of lapsed religion. Meanwhile those who are beginning where he began, disenchanted with the old political categories and anxious to find a way out, must hope that the question of a psychoanalytic understanding of history is not yet closed.

Chapter Three

CONRAD'S UNEASINESS— AND OURS

Two kinds of ideologizing are rejected in this example of applied psychoanalysis. The more manifest quarrel is with those academics, more numerous in 1967 than they are today, who value a writer like Conrad largely for the uplifting sentiments with which he told his psychic rosary. But the essay also declines a "radical" opportunity to use Conrad as the occasion for a lesson in anti-imperialism. Criticism, I thought, should find a deeper level of entry into an author's works than his opinions can provide—especially when his opinions are as murky as Conrad's. Whether my own approach completely avoided another pitfall, that of biographical reductionism, is a question I brushed aside too quickly at the time.

*"Après tout rien ne remplace
les amitiés de notre enfance."*
CONRAD (Letter to Marguerite Poradowska,
October 16, 1891)

*P*redictions about the future ranking of authors should be
made with the greatest tentativeness or not at all. In retrospect
it is easy to see that literary value in any given age has been
glimpsed through a haze of ideology (it wasn't long ago that
By Love Possessed was thought by many to be the Great American Novel). The academy, that home of disinterested taste,
cannot be appealed to as a referee; there a swelling GNP of
discreet praise for every "major author" is bound to be heard,
and one author may be favored over another simply because
he lends himself to a more labored approach. Joseph Conrad is
a case in point: he was trilingual, he was influenced and influential, he did some obscure things that need to be "re-
searched," he studded his works with symbols, and he exuded
a moral portentousness that both invites and resists analysis.
Most "Conradians" would find it hard to separate these professional conveniences from the question of Conrad's ultimate
merit. Those of us who are involved in the quaint modern industry of explaining literature are assailed sometimes by a
doubt as to whether we even know what we like. To say what
some future generation would like is quite beyond our power;
the closest we can come is to try to define for ourselves the
shape and limits of an author's imaginative world.

For Conrad, however, this is evidently a difficult undertaking. Everyone recognizes—in passing—that his fiction is per-
vaded with uneasiness, but something about Conrad urges his
critics to hurry on to the "moral issues" which are taken so
very seriously. One can read a great deal of commentary before coming across any sustained discussion of the wishes and
fears that lie behind his art, energizing it and yet warping it

into something quite distinct from dramatized philosophy or nautical tale-spinning. We are told over and over that Conrad preferred responsibility and discipline to self-indulgence, but what must have been painfully defensive for Conrad somehow comes out sounding merely thematic. The final Conradian gesture, whether of courage or duty or tragic pessimism or human solidarity, gets more of the attention while the mental turmoil that precipitated it gets lip service. What is engaging about Conrad for me and I daresay for others is the part of his imagination that is prior to this withdrawal into gesture—the part that Marvin Mudrick refers to darkly, without explanation, as Conrad's "suppressed . . . nightmares." [1] But it is one thing to sense this fact and another to bring it into critical focus. On the whole the "close analysis" of our time has been devoted not to understanding anxiety but to mollifying it.

A prime instance is F. R. Leavis' widely quoted chapter on Conrad in *The Great Tradition*. Leavis is made uneasy by Conrad's "adjectival insistence upon inexpressible and incomprehensible mystery," [2] but it wouldn't occur to him to inquire *why* Conrad writes this way. He is too busy showing that despite his imperfections Conrad is a great novelist, since he produced "work addressed to the adult mind." What the adult mind seems to approve is a combination of tangible realism (a "vivid essential record, in terms of things seen and incidents experienced by a main agent in the narrative, and particular contacts and exchanges with other human agents . . .") and bracing moralism ("he does believe intensely, as a matter of concrete experience, in the kind of human achievement represented by the Merchant Service—tradition, discipline and moral ideal . . ."). Leavis wants to convince himself that behind the expansive adjectives sit good English nouns, "firm and vivid concreteness" and characters "each having a specific representative moral significance" (Leavis, pp. 272, 215, 242, 237, 232). This clinging to the palpable and the banal is in a curious sense a plausible response to Conrad, who wanted to

see his fiction as Leavis sees it and would have been grateful
for such cooperation.[3] Whereas most critics merely underrate
the atmosphere of guilt and depression that encircles Conrad's
world, Leavis is positively determined to ignore it. His favorite novel, *Nostromo,* has "a certain robust vigour of melodrama
. . . completely controlled to the pattern of moral significance." "There is plainly no room in *Nostromo* for the kind of
illustrated psychology that many critics think they have a right
to demand of a novelist . . ." (Leavis, pp. 240, 238). In short,
there is plainly no room in Leavis for Conrad.

The American academic reply to Conrad's problematic quality is more businesslike and complacent than Leavis': explication replaces value judgment. Take, for example, the three
casebooks in which scholars quarrel politely over what "Heart
of Darkness" truly means. The specific job is to decide
whether Conrad wanted us to be just like his narrator Marlow
or to look down on him as morally inadequate. Since Conrad
was in fact much too involved with Marlow to conceive of either of these cautionary ideas, the issue is agreeably difficult
to settle; recourse must be had to patterns of imagery and
allusion, in which, it is supposed, the author's lessons have
been imbedded. Thus for one critic the allusions to the *Aeneid*
constitute the hidden key; for another it is the allusions to the
Inferno; for another it is the allusions to Buddhism, which
show us some remarkably flattering things about Marlow
which are not even hinted in the literal plot.[4] Depending on
whether they find Marlow a satirized "persona" or a saint, the
critics discern that "Heart of Darkness" is really a grail quest
or a protoexistentialist essay or an attack on Christian hypocrisy or a critique of imperialism. In fundamental respects these
interpretations are alike. All are concerned with some equivalent of salvation—a subject whose appeal these days seems restricted almost exclusively to people on the academic ladder.
All take for granted the greatness and the single-minded didacticism of Conrad's novella. None tries to think of Conrad as

a troubled man who worked amid the prejudices of his age and the exigencies of his own nervous mind. The critics have paid him their highest compliment: he has been graduated from an author to an Assignment.

It should be noted, however, that the most refreshing exceptions to this trend are provided by Americans who share their colleagues' feeling that Conrad's mysteries can be decoded. The pivotal issue is whether Conrad himself grasped the deeper consistencies of his art. In *Joseph Conrad: Achievement and Decline,* Thomas Moser concluded with a certain embarrassed surprise that Conrad's celebrated "later affirmation" makes excellent sense as a pseudoaffirmation, a whistling in the dark. By exposing a disparity between statement and emotional tone, Moser threw into question the whole genteel enterprise of understanding Conrad through his "views." Not surprisingly, Moser's book has been something of a black sheep among Conrad studies, but now it has been confirmed and expanded in many directions by Bernard C. Meyer's *Joseph Conrad: A Psychoanalytic Biography.* It is a telling reflection on literary study today that this book, which aspires merely to say what Conrad personally was like, should provide insights into his fiction that go beyond anything offered by his professional critics. Being a psychoanalyst, Dr. Meyer takes for granted a continuity between the author's psychic life generally and the symbolic world of his fiction; this simple assumption, without which no incisive criticism is possible, has not been drummed out of him by graduate training in "English."

In making Conrad fully and plausibly human for the first time, Dr. Meyer's book will give a jolt to many critics whose readings, though they purport to be independent of biographical trivialities, in fact rely heavily on a sentimental view of the stoical mariner Conrad. It ought to be harder from now on to take this line. The Conrad who recommended stoicism was in his private life a hypochondriac and at times a suicidal defeat-ist; the Romantic lover of the sea was bored to fury whenever he had to pass much time on it; the lover of truth had a way of lying about his past; the defender of chivalry made babyish demands on his wife and resented the existence of his children. Conrad's idolators will have to ponder such incidents as his tossing his infant's clothes out a train window, or his retiring to his room for three weeks when the family maid died and writing melancholy letters from "Your boy" to his wife downstairs. It seems cruel to mention these long-available details of petty behavior, which could probably be matched from any great writer's life, but the cruelty is toward a false image and not toward Conrad, whose dignity consisted precisely in his struggle to overcome his emotional incapacities.

Paradoxically, I suspect that a certain iconoclasm toward the beauty of artists' lives may be conducive to an honest respect for their art. However eager we may be to look up to a novelist for moral guidance, this wish is clearly not what involves and holds us in his fiction. If fiction teaches a lesson it is only as a by-product of something more crucial, a shared experience; not ideas but fantasies entice us into someone else's imaginative world. It is no coincidence that Moser and Meyer, with their interest in aspects of Conrad's work that contradict his deliberate moral intentions, can make better sense of verbal nuances and oddities of plotting than other critics have done. No moral or formal commentary can account for the fact that Conrad's best work, in Mudrick's words, produces an effect of "obstruction and deadlock, an opposition of matched and mutually paralyzed energies" (Mudrick, p. 2). Conrad's most significant level of discourse is the unconscious level, where inadmissible wishes are entertained, blocked, and allowed a choked and guarded expression.

The atmosphere of Conrad's fiction is only partly one of physical challenge; there is always an opposite pull toward easeful death. The source of this urge is obviously his own depressive tendency, which he fought, disguised, and tried to

negate in his art as in his life. And yet he is a consistently autobiographical writer; the effort to shout down his deepest impulses entails an incessant recasting of his psychic history. As
Dr. Meyer points out, "almost without exception Conrad's
heroes are motherless wanderers, postponing through momentary bursts of action their long-awaited return to a mother,
whose untimely death has sown the seeds of longing and re-
morse, and whose voice, whispered from beyond the grave,
utters her insistent claim upon her son's return." [5] The fathers
of these heroes, like Conrad's own father, tend to have out-
lived the mothers for a while and then died or departed, leaving the sons to brood over their intimidating high-mind-
edness and disastrous fanaticism. This concern with the
posthumous grip of the parents amounts to an oblique assign-
ing of blame for the inhibition which characterizes Conrad's
protagonists and is never adequately explained on "realistic"
grounds. Conrad tells us in effect that his characters cannot involve themselves emotionally because they suffer from fixation; they are too busy fending off resentments and longings
toward the departed elders to permit themselves anything
more than the most furtive encounters with their contemporaries.

It is startling to see how all the peculiarities of the Conradian world fall into place in this perspective. Like Hemingway, Conrad wavered between a maudlin *Weltschmerz* and a
defensive assertiveness about the importance of manly style;
the two attitudes are psychologically consistent in that one is
an antidote to the other. The value of action for such a writer
is measured by the inertia that must be overcome to achieve it.
Manhood is always in doubt, and its reconfirmation can only
be made believable in an exclusively masculine ambience
hedged with rules and physical difficulties. Hence the otherwise inexplicable feeling in Conrad that nautical duty and discipline and trial constitute a welcome respite from something
more fearsome. In a word, that something is sexuality. Conrad

can permit himself to imagine a love relationship only if it is a matching of racial opposites—that is, if it contains an alibi to the accusation of being latently incestuous. When the lovers are of similar background they lock themselves in what Dr. Meyer calls a morass of inhibition, "all the while engaging in a ruminative chatter that at times approaches sheer double-talk" (Meyer, pp. 112–113). But Conrad's precautions do not stop there. His heroes, for all their exotic adventures, amount to virtual eunuchs, while his heroines tend to be awesome, androgynous, self-sufficient monoliths who can be fought over but not fertilized. His heroes' mortality rate rises sharply as they approach these Brobdingnagian ladies, who evidently pose a menace more forbidding than any hazard of the male world. Death is at once a symbol of castration and the surest escape from it, a flight from incest and a return to it—and, of course, by killing off his heroes Conrad spares himself the awkwardness of trying to depict love scenes when his mind is possessed by fantasies of this sort.

The critics have been hard pressed to say why Conrad succeeds despite his evasions, which they prefer to minimize. But the question has been wrongly put: Conrad's evasions themselves serve a function within his economy of "mutually paralyzed energies," and criticism should be able to say what the function is. Conrad's uniqueness does not consist in the virtues for which he is most often praised—vivid detail, evocative scenery, suspense, moral concern, a sense of the heroic—but in the fact that he carries these traits along in a nose dive toward self-destruction. He is simultaneously terrified at existence and a connoisseur of its heightened moments, at once a nihilist and a raconteur. This tension is sustained by the "adjectival" rhetoric which looks so foolishly obfuscating when it is extracted for analysis. Even the memorable sentences, the ones that strike us as profoundly true, serve to mediate among Conrad's contrary impulses. Take, for instance, his haunting remark in *Nostromo* that "in our activity alone do we find the sustaining illusion of an independent existence as against the whole scheme of things of which we form a helpless part." That is classic Conrad, not only because it contains a flash of tragic insight but also because it blurs responsibility: to think of oneself as helpless within a metaphysical void is to assign an external cause for one's prevailing depression. I suggest that this quasi-confessional mode is Conrad's forte and that we are more affected by it than we may care to admit. Conrad indulges our fears of isolation, neglect, and victimization by malign higher powers—the fears of an anxious infant— without locating their source. There is something luxurious about the Conradian *Angst;* it comforts us because it is shared, indeed it is built into the order of things, and we combat it with the fellowship of our orphanage. Underlying everything is the seductive, unmentionable thought that it is not so bad after one's fitful strivings to sink back into the maternal nothingness.[6]

This is not to deny what everyone feels, that Conrad is a stoic writer, but rather to identify his chief antagonist as the despairing side of his own mind. The external sources of gloom, "the solitude of the sea" and "the inscrutable eyes of the Most High" (I am quoting the Author's Note to *Almayer's Folly*), are not so much combated as they are sought out as metaphors of preexisting inhibition—and very precise metaphors at that, since psychologically they amount to allusions to the parent figures with whom Conrad is unceasingly involved. The real agon in Conrad is the struggle against inhibition. It is no small point in his favor that he always tried to resist the impulse—indulged, for example, by Henry James—to pretend that his taste for sexless irresolution was a superior achievement of some sort. Every Jamesian plot puts a thick moral varnish on the necessities of the Jamesian temperament, but Conrad did what he could to oppose the passivity which usually has the final say in his works. Common human experience was sacred for Conrad, as it distinctly wasn't for James,

because he grasped at it for rescue from the real destructive element, his instinct for failure.

When this aspect of Conrad's fiction is perceived, he is apt
to appear a psychological ironist, a student of the way the misfortunes of nervous, lonely dreamers are determined, not by
the cruel fates as they imagine, but by their own masochism.
There is evidence for such readings; what is doubtful is that
Conrad expected them. His engagement in his plots would
seem to have more to do with self-exculpation than with dis-
passionate analysis. The semblance of irony is thrown up by
his need to review his misgivings about himself, but when the
misgivings become too insistent they must be replaced by
muddle. Conrad typically diverts our interest from the hero's
gloomy mind to his lush surroundings, which are stocked
with misplaced energies; we expect confessions and instead
we get tropical storms. The very fact that the plots are so
crammed with adventure is comprehensible in this light. The
hero is kept too busy staving off real "savages" and villains to
spare time for self-inquiry, and in most cases we are finally
meant to think of him as a victim of hard luck. Thus Conrad
avails himself of projection—into the landscape, into "the
whole scheme of things of which we form a helpless part"—in
order to blunt an insight which would amount to self-analysis.
Conrad the celebrated realist brings to mind Genet's sardonic
definition of verisimilitude: "the disavowal of unavowable
reasons."

For the comfort of disavowal Conrad pays a price in stereotyped characterization, melodramatic incidents, and the over-
working of exotic props. (The three traits are really one, the
negation of what is complicated, personal, and paralyzing by
what is simple, alien, and active.) Not surprisingly, the works
that have stood up best—nearly all of which were written in
the so-called "Hueffer decade" of 1899–1909, when Conrad felt
himself to have an ally against despair—are those which come
nearest to self-confrontation. In *Lord Jim*, for example, though

it is never stated in so many words that Jim is to be held responsible both for his aberration on the "Patna" and for his passively accepted "punishment" in Patusan, Conrad at least allows us to infer the logic connecting the two parts of the story. By dividing his own mentality into Jim and Marlow, furthermore, he is able to muster a degree of detachment from Jim's tendency to blame external forces for his doom. In contrast, the author of such late novels as *Chance*, *Victory*, and *Suspense* sides with Jim; in Albert Guerard's words, "evil and failure in this new cleansed moral universe are presumed to come from outside rather than from within." [7] Significantly, the most conspicuous change occurs in Conrad's treatment of women. Though he never at any period recognized that misogyny is more an affair of male psychology than of female sin, in his later phase he felt compelled both to idolize womankind and to denigrate it with slanderous generalities, both to try his hand at idyllic love scenes and to wilt them with the abhorrent language studied by Moser. It is evident, as Dr. Meyer has shown in detail, that Conrad's later fiction is ridden by the same mechanisms of denial and projection that came to dominate his psychic life after his total breakdown in 1910—during which, according to Mrs. Conrad, he let loose a "stream of disjointed accusations concerning my moral and spiritual character." [8]

As an example of the way these deep constraints can mar an otherwise promising novel, consider *Victory*. Among critics who take Conrad's "later affirmation" at face value it is regarded as a near masterpiece.[9] Yet the whole novel is built upon an anomaly which Conrad seems unable to control: as the hero gets (verbally) more committed to involvement in the world, his remarkable passivity is not overcome but intensified. In effect Axel Heyst does nothing to defend himself and his mistress Lena from the four villains whose chief business seems to be to persecute him. The atmosphere of muffled depression which has accumulated over many chapters is discharged through a series of weirdly static *tableaux* in which Heyst has no efficient part. This immobility is contagious; the main villain, Jones, turns out to be almost as much a by-stander as Heyst, and what they witness is confusing in the extreme. Whatever passion Conrad had intended to explore is shunted off onto the lecher Ricardo and Lena, who is promoted rapidly from a meek and threatened chorus girl to a typical Conradian Amazon, statuesque and immensely power-ful. She mesmerizes Heyst, Jones is terrified at the thought of her, and the would-be seducer Ricardo addresses her in a way that makes one reach for Krafft-Ebing. "What you want is a man," he tells her, "a master that will let you put the heel of your shoe on his neck." Instead of indicating that there might be something a bit odd about such a relationship, Conrad proceeds to a climactic scene that is perverse in every sense. Lena succeeds in acquiring Ricardo's knife, not to protect her-self but to secrete it between her legs so that "the dreaded thing was out of sight at last," while Ricardo shows the nature of his sexuality by crawling across the room and timidly beg-ging Lena to stick out her foot: "Ricardo, clasping her ankle, pressed his lips time after time to the instep, muttering gasp-ing words that were like sobs, making little noises that resem-bled the sounds of grief and distress." When things have reached such a compromised point it is understandable that Conrad should halt them with a gunshot that seems to have been fired by Heyst but in fact has been fired by Jones, and that seems to have merely wounded Ricardo but in fact kills Lena. No wonder, too, that after this charade the familiar ob-jects of Heyst's room should appear to him "shadowy, unsub-stantial, the dumb accomplices of an amazing dream-plot end-ing in an illusory effect of awakening . . ." [10]

Viewed as fantasy, all the literal peculiarities of *Victory* belong together: the rescue of the mother-Magdalen (that is Lena's name) from a paternal seducer (Schomberg); the flight of the incestuous pair to an island retreat where further ag-

gressors arrive to renew the father's claim; the mother's transformation, under this threat, from ward to protectress, while
the hero-son becomes more infantile; the pseudosolution of
denying female "castration" (Lena's acquisition of the knife,
plus the eroticization of her foot); and a self-immolation that is
meant to cancel all filial presumption. Implausible as these
strategies may sound to "literary" ears, they are common in
Conrad's art—in his life, too, for that matter. But their immediate importance for *Victory* is that they explain its bizarre episodes and Conrad's failure to see how they must strike the
reader. He cannot detach himself adequately from Jones's an-
tifeminine ravings and Ricardo's fetishism because, quite simply, they are his own; all he can do is to foist them off onto exaggeratedly "other" antagonists of his exaggeratedly Christlike
hero. To perceive what Conrad must have been wrestling with
in the act of writing is to see why he repeatedly assures us,
with subtle cavils, of Heyst's respect for his father's memory,
and why Heyst behaves as if he were not so sure of his unim-
peachable right to Lena, and why Lena herself is uncomfortably convincing in her pretense of wanting to abandon Heyst.
The novel's aesthetic incompleteness is a consequence of its
censored self-debate:the details that stand out as blemishes are
coherent only as replies to charges that Conrad has suppressed
in the interest of his dubious tranquillity.

It may be possible now to appreciate the link between
Conrad's artistic freedom and his capacity to manage psychological insight. Given his makeup, he had to deal regularly
with obsessional themes, and he could never distance himself
from them in the manner, say, of Thomas Mann. But he could,
at his best, harmonize them with a plot which was manifestly
"about" a psychic bondage of some sort, even if it had to end
in equivocations. The trouble with *Victory* is that Conrad
wants no part whatsoever of the forces that are tyrannizing
over his plot; the result of his divided purpose is a sulky and
confusing reticence. In all his finest novels and tales he is

moving toward, not away from, a recognition that character is destiny. In these works the charged language, the undercurrent of double entendre which was bound to be present anyway, works with the momentum of the plot, and we are carried through an experience that feels single and whole.

Here, however, Conrad's cultural remoteness from us becomes pertinent. Conrad was on the whole a good Victorian, which is to say that he was earnestly overwrought about maintaining order and decency in his mind, and was apt to mistake the effects of repression for the structure of the universe. Even in his own time he was not a "modern." He lived long enough to call Lawrence's writings "Filth. Nothing but obscenities"; and he used his resonant prose to shore up semblances of the piety which all the great modern writers began by smashing. There was no real choice involved in his continuing to work his customary vein, telling fireside tales of adventure after Joyce and Lawrence and Yeats and Eliot had turned their backs on the philistine public of their day. Conrad and the *hypocrite lecteur* needed each other's company; in order to have access to his creativity he had to believe he was engaged in validating common mankind's good opinion of itself.

His critics, by and large, have shared this opinion, and some have gone so far as to suggest that it is precisely his conventionality that guarantees his stature: Conrad still tells a story, he speaks to Everyman, he still believes in virtue, etc. It is questionable whether this popular reasoning, which ignores everything latent and cherishes the hollowest conscious avowals, really protects Conrad's standing; it seems rather to turn him into the complacent bore he sometimes aspired to be. To put supreme value on obstacles which he set against the deepest current of his art is to forfeit any hope of explaining his power. It would be better to take account of his Victorianism from the beginning, which means above all to recognize that the Conradian experience, while intense and cathartic, is built around taboos that have lost much of their sacredness. Given the Victorian rules of the game, Conrad's grandiose but barely sustained duplicity with himself can be understood as the enabling condition of his narrative energy.

In order to pose this issue concretely, let me return in some detail to "Heart of Darkness," which is surely Conrad at his best. This is not to say that its intellectual content is especially profound or even clear; on the contrary, the one definite point that emerges from the cacaphony of explication is that the appeal of this story cannot rest on its ideas. I suppose it was by working in an irresolute state that Conrad managed to keep the source of his inspiration so extraordinarily open. What matters, in any case, is that nearly everyone can respond to the symbolic experience at the base of his plot and feel the consonance between overt and latent emphasis. As a deliberately "psychological" tale, a pilgrimage toward some debasing revelation about human character, "Heart of Darkness" is not immobilized by totally contradictory intentions in the manner of *Victory*. Marlow tells us explicitly that Kurtz is "the nightmare of my choice," [11] and no subtle inferences are needed to establish his ambivalence toward Kurtz. We see, for example, that he yearns to hear Kurtz's voice but cannot stand to hear of the natives' obeisances to him; we see him hanging on Kurtz's dying words but refusing to approach the corpse or witness its disposal; and we see that he is willing to lie on Kurtz's behalf even though he regards him as a degenerate. It is Marlow himself who finally concludes, "I had no clear perception of what it was I really wanted," and who surmises that he has had an "unconscious loyalty" to Kurtz (*HD*, p. 74). Thus, though we are not meant to decipher exactly what is meant by "the horror," "the fascination of the abomination," and so on—indeed, though Conrad expects us to share Marlow's and his own feeling of being assailed by "something altogether monstrous, intolerable to thought and odious to the soul" (*HD*, p. 65)—we know at least that Marlow's adventure amounts to an uncanny self-unfolding.

No one, to my knowledge, has bothered to define the psychological content of this adventure,[12] but it is hardly obscure. Just consider: a sunken, ascetic narrator who fervently believes that women should be kept quarantined "in that beautiful world of their own, lest ours gets worse," tells us that he felt irrationally compelled to visit a dark and mysterious continent, a "confoundedly big" and "dumb thing," "and I had heard Mr. Kurtz was in there" (*HD*, pp. 49, 27). Since childhood he had yearned to visit this area, and now at great risk and in the face of Kurtz's hostility he arrived via a river described as "an immense snake uncoiled, with its head in the sea, its body at rest curving afar over a vast country, and its tail lost in the depths of the land." After passing jungle of "vengeful aspect" whose rank and matted vegetation appeared ready to "sweep every little man of us out of his little existence," he eventually found the much-respected Kurtz in a state of depravity, accompanied by a savage mistress in a wilderness "that seemed to draw him to its pitiless breast by the awakening of forgotten and brutal instincts, by the memory of gratified and monstrous passions" (*HD*, pp. 8, 34, 30, 67). Now withered and helpless, and rescued by the narrator from "certain midnight dances ending with unspeakable rites" (*HD*, p. 51), Kurtz acknowledged "the horror" of his experience and died, after which the narrator found himself strangely interested in protecting the dead man's reputation—especially in the eyes of a marmoreal, mourning lady who overrated him.

If such a plot were recounted to a psychoanalyst as a dream—and that is just what Marlow calls it—the interpretation would be beyond doubt. The exposed sinner at the heart of darkness would be an image of the father, accused of sexual "rites" with the mother. The dreamer is preoccupied with the primal scene, which he symbolically interrupts. The journey into the maternal body is both voyeuristic and incestuous, and the rescue of the father is more defiant and supplantive than tender and restitutive. The closing episode with the "phantom" woman in a sarcophagal setting would be the dreamer-son's squaring of accounts with his dead mother. He "knows" that parental sexuality is entirely the father's fault, and he has preserved the maternal image untarnished by imagining that the father's partner was not she but a savage woman, a personification of the distant country's "colossal body of the fecund and mysterious life" (*HD*, p. 62). But given the anxiety generated by his fantasy of usurpation, he prefers to suppress the father's misdeeds. Such a tactic reduces the threat of punishment while reestablishing the "pure" mother-son dyad. Only one complaint against the sainted mother is allowed to reach expression: the son tells her with devious truthfulness that the dying sinner's last word ("horror!") was "your name" (*HD*, p. 79).

I do not want to review the abundant evidence that this "dream" is indeed the shaping force in "Heart of Darkness"; this fact will prove if anything too apparent to an unprejudiced reader who goes over the story with attention to its language and the stages of its plot. Derivatives of the primal scene await the hero everywhere: the African bush swarms with "naked breasts, arms, legs, glaring eyes," "a black and incomprehensible frenzy," "a great human passion let loose," "the inconceivable ceremonies of some devilish initiation," and so forth (*HD*, pp. 46, 36, 44, 49). In such surroundings the threat of castration from the two classic sources, the father's wrath and the mother's body, is relentless:

> I avoided a vast artificial hole somebody had been digging on the slope, the purpose of which I found it impossible to divine. It wasn't a quarry or a sandpit, anyhow. It was just a hole. . . . Then I nearly fell into a very narrow ravine, almost no more than a scar in the hillside. I discovered that a lot of imported drainage-pipes for the settlement had been tumbled in there. There wasn't one that was not broken. It was a wanton smash-up. At last I got under the trees. My purpose was to stroll into the shade for a moment; but no sooner within than it seemed to me I had stepped into gloomy circle of some Inferno. . . . (*HD*, p. 17).

To look at such a passage with comprehension of its plentiful symbolic detail is to have removed oneself from Marlow's literal difficulties; the text threatens to become no longer a story but a clinical document.

Conrad specialists have yet to face this eventuality, but their reaction can be predicted. Nothing is more repugnant to most literary scholars than the thought that their favorite author was prey to obscene wishes and worries. When simple incredulity does not dispel the evidence, they attempt a more sophisticated accommodation: "Freudian insights" are welcomed into the roomy mansion of criticism to coexist peacefully with insights of every other sort. Each "meaning" is taken as further testimony to the author's conscious art; if it becomes necessary to recognize that, say, castration anxiety is a feature of the text, then the author can be credited with a prescient exposé of his hero, who is now seen to lack masculinity *and* divine grace. Thus the last and least sincere stand against mental strife is a specious hyper-Freudianism which takes for granted a pre-Freudian writer's conscious manipulation of psychoanalytic categories as if they had been common knowledge all along. By means of such sophistry an aloof, tastefully dehumanized notion of creativity can be upheld while token deference is being paid to the irrational.

Perhaps, then, it is worthwhile to belabor the obvious point that "Heart of Darkness" is in the most agitated sense an autobiographical work. Far from criticizing Marlow, Conrad was using him to recapitulate and try to master the Congo experience he himself had sought out and undergone in 1890—an experience that led not to philosophical conclusions but to a physical and nervous collapse. Conrad's Congo interlude presents exactly the interpretive problem for his biographers that "Heart of Darkness" does for his critics; in both cases he went out of his way to make a real journey coincide with an unconscious investigation of his morbidity. It could be shown that "Heart of Darkness" is packed with family allusions so private that no concept of "conscious art" could make use of them. In various ways Kurtz amounts to a vindictive reconstruction of Conrad's father,[13] and the story alludes not only to the Congo voyage but also to the childhood period of exile in Russia after Conrad's mother, like Kurtz's Intended, had retired to a "sepulchral city" with "an ashy halo," leaving Conrad to cope with a father who inspired what Zdzislaw Najder calls "admiration and contemptuous pity." [14] Then Conrad like Marlow must have "resented bitterly the absurd danger of our situation, as if to be at the mercy of that atrocious phantom had been a dishonouring necessity." [15] Whether or not this cryptic aspect of the story is recognized, it should be clear to everyone that Conrad as well as Marlow is rattled by the idea of Kurtz, who is melodramatically overdrawn and yet scarcely permitted to appear.

In a broader sense we can see that Conrad's involvement in the unconscious allegory of "Heart of Darkness" explains its combination of hallucinatory vividness and garbled ideas. The whole account of European imperialism in the Congo is brilliantly convincing, not because of any developed ideology on Conrad's part, but because in his struggle with Oedipal "savagery" he feels within himself the pathology of men who want both to improve the brutes and to exterminate them. Because he thinks incessantly of usurping the father's power and privilege, he grasps the zeal to lord it within a cutthroat bureaucracy and to "tear treasure out of the bowels of the land" (*HD*, p. 31). No one is better at investing real observations of folly and sadism with the fever of a mind that has already imagined the worst criminality and severest punishment. What he cannot do, however, is relinquish this charmed mood or think clearly about its basis. Since everything that is necessary to Marlow's sanity is necessary to Conrad's, he cannot crawl out of Marlow's mind even for a moment. Hence the difficulty he has in conceiving of the Congolese except as objects of persecution or diabolical headhunters; he too shares the need for bogeymen whose howls and dances will be, not signs of a culture, but simply abominations. He cannot even have Marlow say without hedging that Christianizing the Congo is a mistake, for he still aspires to put down the heathen in himself. In short, Conrad finds no point of repose from which to assess the ordeal he puts us through. All he can muster as a substitute are dabs of moral philosophy—treasured like scripture by his critics—to plaster over his confusion about the causes of his melancholy.

To a certain degree, then, "Heart of Darkness" *is* a clinical document, a record of persisting misery. This is not to deny its power as art but on the contrary to suggest where its power must lie. Despite some details which owe their significance to memories that have not been made available in the text, the anxiety of the whole story comes across unmistakably. We do not yet have an aesthetics of anxiety—indeed, the New-Critical enterprise can be construed as a skirting of the problem, a defensive anchoring of emotion in "objective correlatives" and self-referring tensions—but in reading a deeply ordered work of anxiety we seem willing to concede the suitability of its "adjectival" and "vaporous" language to hidden referents. If we feel "Heart of Darkness" to be somehow coherent despite its patent vagueness and its air of near hysteria, this is because a return of the repressed is not lost on us. We know it is right for Marlow, with his prurient interest in his elders' misdeeds, to be drawn into a journey that leads to knowledge of certain midnight dances ending with unspeakable rites, and on the same level of awareness we know he must make amends for having entertained such a revelation.

I doubt whether any biographical knowledge about "Heart of Darkness" or any critical account of its logic will make its disguised content too available for dramatic illusion to be sustained. Such information only helps to explain why the story seizes us anew with every reading. To say this, however, is not to say that Conrad's sensibility is our own. Nihilism, which in Conrad is surreptitious and nicely padded with scenic effects, has become aggressively explicit in the serious literature of our day, and anyone who prefers Conrad's mode is likely to be conscious of doing so nostalgically. The most awesome and permanent Conradian secrets, the unseen magnets which bind every detail in the field of his plots, are now matter for offhand jokes: "I was on my way to my mother," says Beckett's Molloy, "whose charity kept me dying." [16] A contemporary writer could be forgiven for envying Conrad's relative ignorance, which enabled him to be earnest about fending off vice and to write stories that merge self-realization with believable and intrinsically lively adventures. Nothing is more symptomatic of the present predicament than that Molloy, the man who is wholly at peace with his bodily self, should have nowhere to go but around in a circle on his autoerotic bicycle. Lesser writers than Beckett, having forfeited much of the power of latent reference, are rapidly exhausting the power to shock. Aesthetic complexity would seem to be one of the casualties of desublimation.

If this is so, then we have Conrad's neurosis and the style of his culture to thank, not of course for his genius, but for the special quality of his appeal. In the manuscript of "Heart of Darkness," immediately after Marlow's plea that women be kept apart in their beautiful world, Conrad had added a typically lurid but singularly revealing outburst: "That's a monster-truth with many maws to whom we've got to throw every year—or every day—no matter—no sacrifice is too great—a ransom of pretty, shining lies . . ." (*HD*, p. 49n). That he decided to suppress the remark instead of merely editing out some of its agitation may indicate nothing more than a shrewd assessment of his readership, but that he wrote it in the first place is a mark of his true inner situation. Lying to (and about) women, the quintessential article in the Victorian modus vivendi, was so important to Conrad for his own reasons that he found himself actually putting the requirement into so many words; his curse and opportunity was his need to deal at close range with the gaping monster of his fantasies. Whoever begrudges him his distracting maneuvers has not sufficiently understood the precariousness of the civilized equilibrium he sought to maintain. In retrospect Conrad's lurking skepticism about the strength of conscious decency looks so warranted by public events that we may feel tempted to credit him with a clairvoyant modernity, a vision of general collapse, but precisely because he writhed under the nightmare of history he could not be its interpreter. He did not formulate contradictions, he lived intensely with them and transcribed them into the terms of art. To demand of him something more static and placid, as the bulk of our criticism has implicitly done, is only to manifest in a subtle way what our civilization is now proving with brutal plainness: an incapacity even to imagine what it is like to be human and oppressed.

Chapter Four

ANAESTHETIC CRITICISM

This somewhat belligerent statement was written to introduce *Psychoanalysis and Literary Process,* a collection of essays by Berkeley graduate students. Today I would be more hesitant than I was in 1969 to equate literary meaning with the representation of conflict. Even here, though, less emphasis is placed on the virtues of one method than on the dulling effect of any critical dogma.

*T*he critical essays in this book have in common an overt reference to hypotheses and rules of procedure that were neither derived from literature nor primarily meant to apply to literature. Such criticism can go wrong in several ways: by using weak hypotheses, by using strong and pertinent ones in too mechanical a fashion, or by warping literary evidence to meet presuppositions. The recourse to "extraliterary" theory is not in itself, however, a methodological error. The simple fact that literature is made and enjoyed by human minds guarantees its accessibility to study in terms of broad principles of psychic and social functioning.

This point would seem too obvious to dwell on, but it is widely resisted among the very group to whom it should be most axiomatic, professional students of literature. Most literary scholars observe an informal taboo on methods that would plainly reveal literary determinants. Such methods are considered intrinsically antihumanistic, and criticism systematically employing them is regarded as ipso facto shortsighted. Academic critics often circumvent the taboo by disguising or compromising their explanatory inclination, thus earning a hearing at the expense of some consistency and clarity. But the prohibition itself deserves scrutiny, not only because it is intellectually indefensible but also because its operation has grave consequences for the teaching of literature.

The majority view of deterministic schemes was aptly conveyed by Northrop Frye, one of the most influential of living critics, as he gave assurance that his own theory of literature would not borrow its conceptual framework from sources outside literature itself. Any extrinsic system, he said, gives us, in criticism, the fallacy of what in history is called determinism, where a scholar with a special interest in geography or economics expresses that interest by the rhetorical device of putting his favorite study into a causal relationship with whatever interests him less. Such a method gives one the illusion of explaining one's subject while studying it, thus wasting no time. It would be easy to compile a long list of such determinisms in criticism, all of them, whether Marxist, Thomist, liberal-humanist, neo-Classical, Freudian, Jungian, or existentialist, substituting a critical attitude for criticism, all proposing, not to find a conceptual framework for criticism within literature, but to attach criticism to one of a miscellany of frameworks outside it. The axioms and postulates of criticism, however, have to grow out of the art it deals with. The first thing the literary critic has to do is to read literature, to make an inductive survey of his own field and let his critical principles shape themselves solely out of his knowledge of that field.[1]

Insofar as this statement pleads against replacing sensitive criticism with a crude ransacking of literature to illustrate hypotheses about other matters, it is beyond dispute. More is meant, however. Frye is asserting that the critic, if he is to retain his objectivity, must derive his principles "solely" from his inductive survey of literary works. The point recurs insistently in *Anatomy of Criticism* and is extended into a cautionary view of *all* "axioms and postulates," whatever their source:

There are no definite positions to be taken in chemistry or philology, and if there are any to be taken in criticism, criticism is not a field of genuine learning. . . . One's "definite position" is one's weakness, the source of one's liability to error and prejudice, and to gain adherents to a definite position is only to multiply one's weakness like an infection. (Frye, p. 19)

The modern student of critical theory is faced with a body of rhetoricians who speak of texture and frontal assaults, with students of history who deal with traditions and sources, with critics using material from psychology and anthropology, with Aristotelians, Coleridgeans, Thomists, Freudians, Jungians,

Marxists, with students of myths, rituals, archetypes, metaphors, ambiguities, and significant forms. The student must either admit the principle of polysemous meaning, or choose one of these groups and then try to prove that all the others are less legitimate. The former is the way of scholarship, and leads to the advancement of learning; the latter is the way of pedantry. (Frye, p. 72)

These lines seemingly welcome, but actually discourage, the use of explanatory ideas in criticism. "Polysemous meaning" is recognized only in order to close off the possibility that any one line of investigation might be fruitfully pursued to its end. To have a definite position, no matter how correct, is to be "infected" with weakness, prejudice, and error, whereas to be tolerantly indifferent toward all definite positions, presumably including mistaken ones, is "the way of scholarship." Frye is quite emphatic about this. "All that the disinterested critic can do," when presented with the "color-filter" of an externally derived critical attitude, "is to murmur politely that it shows things in a new light and is indeed a most stimulating contribution to criticism" (Frye, p. 7). Frye himself illustrates his recommendation by glancingly alluding to a variety of frameworks, always with an understanding that they lie beyond the true business of criticism.

Professor Frye's widely accepted imperative, *Do not stray outside literature,* must be seen as territorial rather than intellectual. The avowed idea is to avoid indebtedness to other people's specialties, "for in that case the autonomy of criticism would . . . disappear, and the whole subject would be assimilated to something else" (Frye, p. 6). Once this apprehension is grasped, one can predict the degree of Frye's actual hospitality toward different lines of study. Works can, for example, be safely classified according to their patent resemblances and differences, but in order to say how those features came into being we would have to talk about motives, and there would be no assurance that the motives in question would prove properly "literary." Beneath, let us say, the urge to write an epic or a masque we might come across other urges at once more private and more universal than the literary taxonomist could account for. Thus it is not surprising that Frye repeatedly admonishes the disinterested critic to beware of all psychological explanations.

But this causal vacuum cannot be sustained; a critic who forswears deterministic thinking will inevitably fall back on a covert, wishful determinism bordering on tautology. In Frye's case this is particularly clear. "Poetry can only be made out of other poems," he says, "novels out of other novels. Literature shapes itself, and is not shaped externally . . ." (Frye, p. 97). "The true father or shaping spirit of the poem is the form of the poem itself, and this form is a manifestation of the universal spirit of poetry . . ." (Frye, p. 98); ". . . the central greatness of *Paradise Regained*, as a poem, is . . . the greatness of the theme itself, which Milton *passes on* to the reader from his source" (Frye, p. 96; italics in original); "the real difference between the original and the imitative poet is simply that the former is more profoundly imitative" (Frye, p. 97). Literature makes literature which makes literature; tradition itself is the fount of all inspiration and value. No questions need be asked about how the world's great stories gained their appeal, for the stories themselves are motivational forces. Indeed, Frye dares to hope that even the idea of the Oedipus complex will someday be exposed as nothing more than a misplaced compliment to the power of the Oedipus story: perhaps we shall decide "that the myth of Oedipus informed and gave structure to some psychological investigations at this point. *Freud would in that case be exceptional only in having been well read enough to spot the source of the myth*" (Frye, p. 353; italics added).

This vision of literature as its own progenitor is very far from being a unique indulgence. It is, in fact, a common fantasy among writers, a wish that art could be self-fathered, self-nurturing, self-referential, purified of its actual origins in discontent; and it is no less common among critics. Frye found a use for it in his brilliant study of Blake, virtually annihilating his identity as a critic while fusing himself with Blake's obscure private reality.[2] In that case a rapt surrender to the poet's wish for total imaginative control over the world provided an opportunity for valuable clarification. But such reverence for the all-sufficient text is obviously too narrow a foundation for a whole theory of criticism, and when Frye turns lawgiver he ends by providing an apology for more timid work, indeed for the most routine academic drudgery.

It is important to see that such a result is dictated by the very project of severing literature from its determinants. As Murray Krieger has shown, Frye follows the Arnoldian and Eliotic line of argument which makes artistic unity a substitute for the lost religious matrix, and which decides that in an age of dissociated sensibility this unity must be propped by a body of consciously appropriated belief.[3] Frye's novelty is to fortify the supposedly "anagogic" universe of a poem, not with overt dogmas, but with the rest of literature itself, considered as a great phalanx of works aligned by genre and period. The receding sea of faith has at least left *this* much behind. But as Freud said of Dostoevsky's final piety, lesser minds have reached the same position with less effort. Frye's emphasis on the autonomy of tradition and his simple equation of merit (as in *Paradise Regained*) with borrowed thematic content are all too congenial to critics who could never have written a page of *Fearful Symmetry*. While few professors would say outright that "literature shapes itself," fewer still have ventured beyond the confines of tradition and convention. Indeed, the fear of "going too far" with any hypothesis about literature has proved considerably stronger than the fear of arriving nowhere. Frye's suggestion that Freud himself may have made his name through motif-spotting, a talent we already encourage in our literary trainees, must be reassuring to scholars who would prefer not to raise any awkward questions.

Most literary curricula seem to rest on the assumption, implicit throughout *Anatomy of Criticism,* that the scholar-critic need only become conversant with a certain list of primary and secondary texts in order to begin contributing to knowledge. He should of course be trained in rhetoric and bibliography, but no mention is made of interpretive procedures for bringing some order into the wildly variant subjective responses evoked by any given work. Though first-rate critics like Wilson, Empson, Trilling, and Burke have not hesitated to make "extraliterary" sense of literature, the idea that we positively *ought* to do so is conceived as a threat to scholarly balance. The critic already knows what he is doing and will be all right if he can just keep himself from being drawn too much toward either what Frye has called "the myth of concern" or "the myth of detachment." (It was left for Northrop Frye to identify and endorse the ultimate English-department stance, detachment from the myth of detachment.)

Professor Frye claims that the mental process involved in literary criticism "is as coherent and progressive as the study of science," and he expects that his colleagues' efforts will be revealed as a unified scientific system, "the main principles of which are as yet unknown to us" (Frye, pp. 10–11). This discovery would, as he says, "certainly be convenient" (Frye, p. 11), and many academics will forgive him for going on to treat it as already established. Unfortunately, there seems to be no objective basis for this optimism. The history of literary study is transparently a history of intellectual and political fashion, never more so than in recent formalism and neo-religious moralism. Critics have arrived at no agreement whatever about the meaning of beauty, the criteria of value, or even the grossest facts about books and authors, such as whether Shakespeare was or wasn't stoical, whether Milton was or wasn't of the Devil's party, whether Blake was crazy or visionary or both, whether *The Golden Bowl* is an example of self-transcendence or of colossal arrogance and evasion. Unless one had decided in advance to find criticism "coherent and progressive," he would be hard pressed to justify calling it an intellectual discipline at all.

Such a justification would have to show that literary study, like other disciplines, is concerned with the differential evaluation of various styles of inquiry according to their relative success in making sense of the objects studied. But not only is this winnowing process singularly missing from criticism, it is condemned outright as needlessly zealous, intolerant, and unliterary. Each critic is free to adopt the "approach" that suits his fancy, and most of the approaches prove to be little more than analogical vocabularies lending an air of exactitude to whatever the critic feels like asserting. This is precisely why Professor Frye can urge us not to "choose one . . . and then try to prove that all the others are less legitimate." What does it matter whether we call ourselves Thomists or Aristotelians or phenomenologists, provided we don't take our method too solemnly or show impatience with our neighbor's? *Anatomy of Criticism* is in part a book of professional etiquette, expressing and inculcating the civility that makes literary eclecticism possible. That this civility is in practice anti-intellectual has gone unnoticed—a fact that begins to suggest the extent to which "English" has deafened itself to criteria of knowledge.

The tolerance of literary scholars for "polysemous meaning" is understandably strained by methods that claim to deal in causes and effects. It disappears altogether as soon as such a method is applied in earnest. A critic can allude to Marx now and then, but he had better not get too interested in exposing the class apologetics in cherished texts, much less in other critics' theories of meaning. Similarly, it is a badge of broadmindedness to season a conventional argument with references to Freud, but the references will be calmly received only if they remain honorific. One may, to be sure, safely credit an author (even a pre-Freudian one) with having made use of "Freudian insights." This is not psychoanalytic discourse but a subtle prophylaxis against such discourse, for the fantasy materials that a Freudian would have ascribed to the unconscious source of the work itself have been promoted to the realm of conscious art, where all of us feel at home. To say that an author has endowed his hero with Freudian traits is no more psychoanalytic a statement than to say that he has evoked a pleasant landscape; in both cases the question of unconscious influence over the whole text is being avoided. And this avoidance is the minimal condition a critic must fulfill if he doesn't want to be regarded as unbalanced.

Thus there is less Freudian criticism extant than one might think, and most of it continues to be received either with hostile alarm or with those polite murmurs that Professor Frye advises us to utter in the presence of the single-minded. The reasons for this reception overlap with those explaining the virtual ban on Marxian analysis. Both Freud and Marx ask us to think about matters that not only partake of alien disciplines, but are profoundly unsettling in their own right. While Freud may seem politically less iconoclastic than Marx, his method is in one sense more radical; it leaves the critic with less ground on which to strike a righteous attitude. Psychoanalytic principles bring into question the very possibility that a critic's relation to his texts could be fundamentally rational and disinterested.

Resistance to such self-appraisal assumes many forms, but it almost never assumes the form of meeting Freudian propositions on evidential grounds. From Wellek and Warren's icy and confused chapter on "Literature and Psychology" in 1949 to the present day, it is next to impossible to find a clear and informed discussion of psychoanalysis by a critic who does not employ it.[4] One hears instead that the Freudian revolution was won long ago and that we needn't make a fuss over it

now, or that psychoanalysis has been replaced by any number
of better systems, or that it neglects creativity or communication or religion or society or existential anguish or aesthetic textures. Such half-truths are usually followed by a retreat to homespun moralized psychology or to nebulous,
dignified, quasi-metaphysical concepts such as Jung's, which,
far from seeking to "explain" religion and art, seek to declare
their sublime immunity from explanation.

Indeed, Jung has proved a godsend for many critics troubled
by the menace of psychoanalysis, for he spent the better part
of a lifetime coping with that menace in seductive and readily
adaptable ways. Even someone who applies Jung's system
with unfashionable explicitness and persistence will find himself free to retain an elevated notion of literature. To invoke
that system is of course a revealing mark of indifference toward evidence, for as Edward Glover demonstrated, Jung's hypotheses are logically unnecessary and mutually contradictory;
his methodological stance shifted continually between claims
of adherence to the strictest clinical principles and claims of
rapport with ineffable mysteries; and for these reasons and
others his version of neo-Platonism has made scant impact on
any field of serious inquiry.[5] These, however, are points of
small concern to the lapsed-religious humanist, whose own
hopeful guesses about the uplifting value of literature are as
fanciful as Jung's. Modern men in search of a soul can make
wide allowance for one another's poetic leaps of faith.

This is not to say that critics who openly espouse Jungian-
ism will escape the disapproval of their more cautious colleagues. The latter, failing to appreciate the circularity of
Jung's mental journey, its intent of rescuing spiritual and cultural matters from destructive scrutiny, will find in the use of
Jungian terms yet another instance of going too far. But because the offense is not so much empirical as social, it can be
forestalled merely by using Jung's ideas without attribution or
with suitable disclaimers. Token gestures of skepticism can

become a means of escape from considerations of plausibility—as, for example, in Professor Frye's statement that the collective unconscious is "an unnecessary hypothesis in literary criticism" (Frye, p. 112), even while he has been developing an immanent and impersonal notion of creativity that seems to demand that very hypothesis.

Since good criticism appears to be largely a matter of sympathy, sensitivity, and pertinent learning, one might reasonably ask whether such vagueness over theory has much importance. Yet it does not seem too venturesome to propose that all scholars, even literary ones, could profit from being clear about what they believe and what they are doing. There is also a possibility that what many of them are doing is wrong both in its premises and in its educational impact. Behind the public façade of eclecticism there may lie a dogmatic avoidance of unacknowledged aspects of literary experience; behind the tactful withdrawal from theories, a disregard for knowledge; behind the celebration of traditional themes, an intolerance toward students who want to come to grips with their deepest responses.

These possibilities are in fact widely realized. The cardinal features of professional critical training as most of us know it are a suppression of affect and a displacement of attention from artistic process onto motifs, genres, literary history (conceived not as the study of how books are influenced by objective conditions, but as chronology, borrowings, gossip, and a disembodied "history of ideas"), and the busywork of acquiring the skills and attitudes needed for circumspect research.[6] Actual criticism, in the familiar sense of making a case for the superiority of some works to others, is frowned upon as amateurishly subjective. Since sheer acquaintance with the body of Anglo-American literature is supremely valued, emphasis is laid on "working up" the designated genres and periods without concern over how literature moves us. As Professor Frye says with some enthusiasm, after showing how we can trace

the devices of pastoral elegy from the Bible and the early
Church and Theocritus and Vergil through Sidney, Spenser,
Shakespeare, Milton, Shelley, Arnold, Whitman, and Dylan
Thomas, "we can get a whole liberal education simply by
picking up one conventional poem and following its archetypes as they stretch out into the rest of literature" (Frye,
p. 100).[7]

One could hardly wish for a more vivid statement of the
prevailing academic faith; all that need be added is that no-
body believes it except those who propagate it. By now the
humanizing pretensions of traditional literary study seem to
have been questioned by everyone but its official custodians.
But so long as the field prizes gentility over principled inquiry, no critique of those pretensions is likely to make much
headway; one always runs against the tacit agreement that cu-
rators of culture needn't bother with ideas except as in-
dulgences of taste or fashion.

At present it is generally true that students who reject this
consensus must either feign acceptance of it or drop out of
school. The survivors and inheritors of literary training tend to
be those best adapted to dull, safe, provincial work, while the
more creative and inquisitive students, having squandered
valuable years on the graduate regimen expecting that it *must*
have something to do with the life of the imagination, are
mastered at last by despair.[8] Nor is the despair confined to
students. The occupational disease of "English," rarely acknowledged until recently, is a debilitating fear that literary
scholarship as we have been practicing it is a useless and elitist pastime. If the fear is somewhat exaggerated, the exaggerat-
ion nevertheless springs from an entirely understandable bad
conscience.

II

The answer, then, to the question whether it is antihumanistic
to look outside literature for principles of literary under-

standing must be a further question: What is meant by humanism? The humanism that purports to defend classical and Judeo-Christian values by cherishing the texts in which those values supposedly reside is indeed jeopardized by extraliterary knowledge, but such a humanism amounts to little more than the confusion of a book list with an education, and its practical results are hardly worth preserving. Suppose, however, humanism were taken to mean a concern for knowing (and protecting) man as an evolved species, embarked on a unique and possibly self-abbreviated experiment in the substitution of learning for instinct. In that case there would be no need to build walls between one discipline and all others out of fear that the alleged autonomy of one's specialty might be challenged. On the contrary: the search for universals underlying all cultures and traditions would be everyone's business, and proof that one category of human production, such as literature, is functionally consistent with others would be welcomed as significant.

The starting point of this humanism might be a comparison of man to the nearest primates. Such a comparison seems at present to indicate that man's emergence was accompanied by the suppression of much of his forerunner's patterned behavior, the prolongation of his infantile dependency, the postponement of his sexual maturity but also a rich complication and intensification of his sex life, and the diversion of part of this heightened sexuality into substitutive aims and bonds. The delay and detour of instinctual discharge, while not in themselves an explanation of man's capacity to form concepts and modify his behavior experientially, are almost certainly preconditions for it; yet this same interference with animal function dooms man to self-disgust and neurosis, even making normal mating a precarious achievement for him. Each individual must recapitulate for himself, as if it had never been done before, the species' accommodation to social discipline, and this accommodation is always grudging, never finally settled before the moment of death. A true appreciation of man's

works would take note of the renunciations and risks they
inevitably entail.

Many lines of study could contribute to such an appreciation, but the postulates of Freudian psychoanalysis would be
bound to command interest, for they alone have weighed the
motivational effects of man's emergence as a species.[9] This
was not Freud's original intent, but it was what he stumbled
upon, with a disoriented retreat to fabulous reasoning, when
he grasped the astonishing sameness of the repressed unconscious across all recorded eras and civilizations. Whatever its
therapeutic or even its conceptual disadvantages, only psychoanalysis has registered the psychic costs involved in man's
prolonged dependency and his improvising of culture out of
thwarted desire.

Man, in a Freudian view, is the animal destined to be
overimpressed by his parents, and neurosis is comprehensible
as "abnormal attachment to the past." [10] Freud discovered that
human beings can neither freely accept nor freely deny the
parental demand that sexual and aggressive urges be tamed.
All men, he saw, struggle not only against unregenerate impulses but also against their guilt for continuing to harbor
those impulses. The fantasies and modes of infantile striving
corresponding to the earliest experiences of nutrition, social
training, and genital assertion are never wholly overcome and
are reactivated when later crises strain the adaptive resources
that have been pieced together through a trauma-marked development. It is not so much man's mortality as his inability to
keep from being haunted by his repressed longings that makes
him "a baby who is afraid of being left alone in the dark." [11]
The prevalence of mass as well as individual delusion, the tendency of groups to unleash murderous hostility against other
groups that have been projectively designated as embodying
banished wishes, the orgies of ascetic penance and the rages
for spiritual or material perfection that occupy much of recorded history exemplify the more general rule that men, tor-

mented by the persistence of what they have forsworn, necessarily *regress together*.[12] They do so at their best as well as at
their worst. A pooling of fantasies to impose bearable contours
on the world seems to be a minimal requisite for all human
achievement, even the achievement of those who work alone.
By sanctioning certain regressions a culture enables its
members to *reculer pour mieux sauter.*

This perspective indicates that the primary function of art
may not be instructive or decorative or sedative. Originating
in what Ernst Kris called a "regression in the service of the
ego," [13] art uses symbolic manipulations to reconcile competing pressures. The artist is someone who provisionally relaxes
the censorship regnant in waking life, forgoes some of his society's characteristic defenses, and allows the repressed a measure of representation, though (as in strictly unconscious
symptom formation) only in disguised and compromised
form. His social role and his own equilibrium dictate a sign of
victory for the ego, if not in "happy endings" then in the
triumph of form over chaos, meaning over panic, mediated
claims over naked conflict, purposeful action over sheer psychic spillage. In this sense the making and the apprehension
of art works reenact the entire human project of making a ten-
uous cultural order where none existed before.

Assuming for the moment that this view is right, we can see
that much "impersonal" literary criticism and theory tends to
isolate and redouble the defensive activity in literature while
ignoring its barely mastered elements of fantasy, desire, and
anxiety. A criticism that explicitly or implicitly reduces art to
some combination of moral content and abstract form and
genre conventions is literally an anaesthetic criticism. It insulates the critic and his readers from a threat of affective distur-
bance—a threat that is perfectly real, for there is no reason to
suppose that a reader's ego will prove more flexible and capa-
cious than the artist's was. All literary criticism aims to make
the reading experience more possible for us, but anaesthetic

criticism assumes that this requires keeping caged the anxieties that the artist set free and then recaptured. The effect is often to transform the artist from a struggling fellow mortal into an authority figure, a dispenser of advice about virtue and harmony. "They all swear by the name of the great invalid," Thomas Mann said of any major writer's admirers, "thanks to whose madness they no longer need to be mad." [14]

Someone who wants to look more closely into literature's buried contest between impulse and inhibition will require a method for interpreting his own responses. As a richly overdetermined compromise formation, an art work can only be obliquely and dialectically truthful; so, too, our reaction to it will be a compromise demanded not only by the work's conflicting signals but also by the habitual bias of our ego. The nearest approximation to critical objectivity would seem to consist of gauging those factors both theoretically and intimately and of applying in reverse the principles by which artistic effects came about. This involves open preconceptions about psychic structure, disposition, and defenses and an expectation that certain thematic strands will prove important to follow because of their probable roots in early psychic development. Perhaps the key anticipation of psychoanalytic criticism is that art will borrow some of its real internal unity from repressed material, which "proliferates in the dark" in producing linked derivatives. [15]

Such preconceptions can of course be stigmatized as reductionistic, but all systematic research is comparably governed; the only logical way of getting beyond commonsense impressions is to sharpen one's focus and then see whether new evidence has come into view and an intelligible order has been revealed. To apply deep-structural rules to literary analysis is no more intrinsically reductionistic than to apply them to the study of language. [16] The establishing of predictable patterns can become a basis for showing the intelligibility of expressions that seemed inert and arbitrary because the wrong questions were being asked about them. Thus the validation of a psychoanalytically oriented criticism rests on whether, at its best, it can make fuller sense of literary texts than could the most impressive instances of a rival criticism.

The likelihood of this result rests on the psychoanalytic anticipation that even the most anomalous details in a work of art will prove psychically functional. Being at bottom a theory of how conflicting demands are adjusted and merged, psychoanalysis is quite prepared for literature's mixed intentions, dissociations of affect from ideational content, hints of atonement for uncommitted acts, bursts of vindictiveness and sentimentality, and ironies that seem to occupy some middle ground between satire and self-criticism. In much literary commentary such phenomena are either overlooked or treated as nuisances to be forgiven or condemned, yet they are pervasive. ("A novel," said Randall Jarrell, "is a prose narrative of some length that has something wrong with it." [17]) The fact that we can be moved by literary elements that are rationally incoherent or formally clumsy is puzzling to the nonpsychoanalytic commentator—so much so that T. S. Eliot, finding no adequate manifest referent for the clogged emotionality he perceived in *Hamlet,* reluctantly declared the play an artistic failure. Freudian discussion, by contrast, can locate the universality of the play's appeal and show how its very indirection, paralysis, and strangely overcharged language are enlisted in the task of coping with a powerful, relatively unelaborated Oedipal fantasy.[18]

Of course such a demonstration can never be more convincing than the reader wants it to be. Although psychoanalysis is not the wholly self-validating system described by some of its detractors,[19] the very nature of its attempt to interpose metaphorical psychic agencies between unconscious activity and overt behavior renders it unamenable to logical proof. Only those of its concepts that are closest to naked observation can be experimentally tested, and the few experiments thus far undertaken, while generally supportive of the theory, hardly close off alternative interpretations.[20] The skeptic is free to say, with the instrumentalists, that Freudian theory is unscientific because its assertions cannot be verified; or to join the positivists who relegate emotive matters to the harmless and meaningless realm of "poetic truth"; or to take refuge among the behaviorists who ensure that nothing so complex and uncontrolled as a human mind can become an object of their attention. All these versions of what C. Wright Mills called "abstracted empiricism"[21] shrug off the conclusions of psychoanalysis instead of attempting to replace them with better ones.

Unfortunately, Freud's achievement is entangled in an embarrassingly careless scientific tradition. The slowness of psychoanalysis to purge itself of unsubstantiated folklore and outmoded concepts cannot be denied. We no longer hear much about the primal crime, phylogenetic memory traces, Eros and Death, the Nirvana principle, or the infant's "primal hating" of the world, but we still find analysts deriving character traits solely from the vicissitudes of drives, dealing in hydraulically conceived sums of libido, and reifying Freud's oversimple tension-discharge model.[22] The virtual hibernation of psychoanalysis during the current period of revolutionary gains in natural science is cause for dismay. Yet there is no rival set of concepts covering the important ground that Freud appropriated seventy years ago. The literary student can hardly undertake a revision of clinical theory, but for the present he must try to ascertain which are its most essential and best verified points.

The main uncertainty facing a Freudian critic, however, is procedural rather than theoretical. The very abundance of "Freudian materials" in literature prompts him to ask what he should make of them, and here the theory cannot tell him which way to turn. Is the artist sicker, or is he better off, than those of us who observe his regressive forays at a distance?

Nothing is easier than to "prove," using certain of Freud's premises, that art is a purely symptomatic activity, or to "prove" with equally Freudian premises that "the artist is not neurotic." The truth is that a literary critic is in a disadvantageous position for making such judgments. A text may open its fantasy life to him but it cannot, like an analyst's patient, react to his presence or delve for still hidden evidence that would support or refute his interpretive hunches. Indeed, because the regressiveness of art is necessarily more apparent to the analytic eye than its integrative and adaptive aspects are, psychoanalytic interpretation risks drawing excessively pathological conclusions. When this risk is put together with the uncertainties plaguing metapsychology itself, one can see why Freudian criticism is always problematic and often inept.

This point has not been lost on psychoanalytic theorists of literature, who have looked for ways of putting Freudian discussion on a sounder logical and empirical basis. The results to date, however, have been somewhat quixotic. The only apparent means of ensuring against the literary equivalent of "wild analysis" is to suppress all interest in pathology, bypass ambiguities of theory, and concentrate on a circumscribed range of evidence. But as soon as this exchange of investigative freedom for a higher degree of certainty has been made, a trivialization seems to occur, and some of the spirit of psychoanalysis is lost. The very routine of one's method becomes a barrier to the deep involvement that should energize all criticism, Freudian criticism above all.

Not even the most coherent and ambitious attempt at a Freudian aesthetics, Norman N. Holland's *The Dynamics of Literary Response*,[23] avoids this pitfall. Holland assumes that literature, on the analogy of the dream and the joke, is essentially understandable as the disguising and discharging of an infantile fantasy—not, however, in the author's mind, which he deems too conjectural to bother with, but only in the reader's. "Literature transforms our primitive wishes and fears into significance, and this transformation gives us pleasure" (Holland, p. 30). If this is so, then something approaching scientific accuracy appears within the reach of criticism, for psychoanalysis tells us much of what we need to know about the two most relevant categories of understanding, namely fantasies and mechanisms of defense. Holland develops a theoretical model that does succeed in differentiating among our responses to various kinds of literature, from entertainments to works of calculated absurdity; this is a substantial contribution. Yet the effect is to promote a predictable form of discussion geared to the model's limited scope. Glossaries of readers' fantasies and defenses, illustrations of their possible combinations, and proof that any work can be assigned a spot in the scheme do not capture the literary enterprise much better than manuals of sex postures capture love. In both cases the inadvertently fostered attitude is resignation: Here we go again, what will it be this time?

This objection does not arise from the common but unreasonable demand that a theory "feel like" what it describes; all theories are of necessity abstract. The quest for total certainty, however, seems to inhibit the first requisite of good criticism and good psychoanalysis, the capacity to be moved. A literary work may impress us with a complexity and economy, an energy and restraint, a precision and reverberation whose ultimate reference is not simply to the "nuclear fantasy" correctly isolated by Holland, but to the whole state of mind evoked by the text. Instead of presenting a disguised infantile wish that acquires "significance," great literature typically invites us to undergo a symbolic process of self-confrontation in which infantile solutions are resisted even as they are indulged. We identify with the pain as well as with the release involved in this process. "Beauty," as Rilke said, "is nothing but the beginning of terror that we are still just able to bear." [24] A criticism that cheerfully catalogues the unconscious tricks we play on ourselves and equates literary power with a judicious recipe of wishes and tactics, introjection and intellection, cannot avoid becoming a new version of anaesthesia—a version using Freud's terminology but lacking Freud's sympathy for the way great artists court unconscious engulfment in order to recreate the conditions of a human order.

This is to say that literature registers and arouses conflict, and that no theoretical preparation can spare a critic the necessity of submitting himself to that conflict. Norman Holland would, I am sure, agree with this statement, yet in practice he empties psychic defenses of their shame and anxiety and treats them much like the formal devices of rhetoric. When this is combined with ground rules discouraging biographical inquiry and value judgments, psychoanalytic discussion becomes what Holland has called "The Next New Criticism," a mere consolidation and deepening of the formalistic close reading of recent decades.[25] Such a tactful presentation seemingly makes room for us Freudians in the kingdom of polysemous meaning, but in actuality no one is placated. Conventional scholars remain quite aware that psychoanalysis constitutes a threat to their style of reading, and they are scandalized by the very claims (for instance, that literature is after all much like joke-telling) by which Holland hopes to make Freudian criticism seem more agreeable.

Freudian criticism can become generally agreeable only by disavowing the idea of unconscious causation. Holland would never do this; he simply avoids authors' minds [26] and keeps his Freudianism well-mannered by showing magnanimity toward the shortcomings of "English." Yet those shortcomings must be directly challenged if "the connection between knowledge and the zest of life" [27] is to be preserved. Psychoanalysis would be yet another scholastic distraction from art if it were assimilated to the current ethos of academic departments. To move from collecting pastoral elegy motifs to collecting instances of phallic mothers would be a smaller step than most professors could imagine, a mere exchange of one indifferent taxonomy for another. The real value of literary psychoanalysis is that it can embolden us to be alone with books, to recognize our own image in them, and from that recognition to begin comprehending their hold over us.

The represented mind to which we respond in literary experience is not precisely the one we could infer from biographical data, but is improvised from what Keats called negative capability. This capability, however, is temperamentally limited by the persisting conflicts that must be managed in any creative process. The ego state suffusing the work must borrow heavily from the "countercathected system"—that is, the cluster of defenses preventing inadmissable actions and expressions—that makes up the author's habitual character, and his career will escape redundancy only to the degree that he can vary his defenses. So, too, our ability to participate will rest on whether we can afford to trade part of our character armor for an imagined equivalent. Fear of psychic dissolution, of surrender to the repressed, is thus the paramount obstacle both to creative freedom and to a reader's capacity for involvement.

It is in this light that we can grasp the significance of fixed genres, with their coded assurance that psychic activity will be patterned and resolved along familiar lines; the genre itself is a ready-made countercathected system. For this very reason, however, art that strives for originality is always restless within its formal borders and frequently generates new forms, which imitators are bound to misunderstand as embodying permanently valid principles of beauty.[28] While the works favored by posterity are not invariably those that defy tradition, their traditional elements always prove to have been adapted to a new vision of reality. This point is familiar in nonpsychological criticism; what psychoanalysis can show is that the new vision amounts to a reconciling of competing claims so as to fuse perception with the expression of conflict.

Criticism starting from an infantile fantasy instead of from this task of reconciliation will not be able to do justice to the cognitive aspect of literature, which is just as "psychoanalytic" as fantasy itself. The crucial difference between literary creation and symptom formation resides in the extra demand we make of literature, that it confirm and extend our sense of truth. Whereas symptoms are rigidly stereotyped, are usually accompanied by guilt, and subtract from an individual's rapport with his surroundings, in the highest literary enjoyment we feel that our pleasure is being sanctioned by reality itself, whose principles have been set for us. This is an illusion, but the illusion can be practiced only by artists whose perceptiveness has not been obliterated by ego needs. A work that flouts our conscious intelligence, as symptoms do, may have an "escape" interest but will be soon rejected for its crudeness or empty conventionality.

To recognize the importance of cognition is not, of course, to say that doses of unadulterated social or historical truth are found in literature and account for its power. Neutral-seeming literary material always conveys unconscious apologetics, and the latter turn out to be more compelling than any amount of faithful description. Hence the shallowness of criticism that evaluates books by their correspondence to approved political facts, and hence the folly of assuming that literature naïvely mirrors the conditions of the age in which it was written. Whatever historical knowledge we can glean from literature is knowledge of the way objective circumstances were apprehended by one sensibility at the sufferance of all other psychic demands. This awareness can be illuminating once its restricted province is understood, but here again the proper point of vantage is neither fantasy nor facts, but the negotiating ego.[29]

Regarded psychoanalytically, literary works are very far from being simple lessons or exhortations decked out in poetic language; yet they *are* messages of a cryptic and intricate sort. Since our common plight is to be forever seeking acquittal from the fantasy-charges we have internalized as the price of ceasing to be infants, we share an eagerness for interpsychic transactions that seem to promise such an acquittal, or at least an abatement of guilt by means of establishing a confessional bond. Rather than being merely an unconscious release within the author or a similar release within the reader, literary process establishes a transitory complicity between the two. The forms this tie can assume are various. Milton's sensuality is hedged with law while Keats's is proclaimed as an imperious right, but both authors are posing ways for us to assert a measure of libidinal freedom. Swift implicates us in his aggression while Hemingway asks us to believe that life is castrating; both allow us to feel that our misanthropic sentiments are neither so unique nor so unfounded as we might have feared. Stendhal admits to a certain hypocrisy but easily wins our agreement that this is the way of the world; Joyce's Stephen tells us that his, and our own, creative ego must brush every hindrance from its path. In each instance we are invited, not to experience a fantasy, but to share a posture toward questionable impulses, and in the act of sharing to diffuse responsibility and stake out some unconscious territory free from the taxation of conscience.

Among the countless possibilities for literary exchange, one relationship seems frequent enough to merit special emphasis. An author often places his reader in the role of parent and begs his absolution. By revealing what has been on his mind, mixing oblique confession with a reassertion of commitment to decency and reality and beauty, and by involving the reader in everything he discloses, the author claims the right to be accepted as he is. But since everyone remains filial on the deep level where literature is registered, the reader does not use the communication quite as it was meant; he welcomes the represented self-exculpation, not as applying to someone else, but as a subtle brief in his own defense.

The tendency of critics to exaggerate the moral, social, or realistic content of literature becomes more comprehensible in this light. Every critic is first a reader who turns the text to the purposes of his beleaguered ego. By transmuting the author into a paragon of conscience or documentary literalism he completes the covering of his tracks; the literary self with which he has identified has been placed beyond reproach. Not even psychoanalytic theory, with its open attention to such unconscious tactics, is a sufficient preventative against their use. By bottling and labeling the repressed contents that Freud thought were so noxious, a Freudian can preclude the self-risk that literature asks of us. Literary art is then revealed as benign parlor magic and nothing more.

"The charm of knowledge would be small," said Nietzsche, "were it not that so much shame has to be overcome on the way to it." [30] Any system of propositions tends eventually to dissipate that shame, either by evading anxiety-provoking matters or by assimilating them to the sense of the ordinary. The latter course is obviously preferable if a choice must be made, yet knowledge about literature has a curious way of ceasing to be wholly true when such a regularization has been accomplished; the loss of uncertainty is also a loss of humanity. This is the kernel of truth in the widespread but largely foolish worry that psychoanalysis will "ruin" our favorite books. While literature is not so easily destroyed by critical remarks, any critic can temporarily make an engaging text seem dreary—not, however, by revealing too much of it, but by revealing too little and claiming this to be the whole. The very success of psychoanalytic theory in anticipating predictable aspects of literature leaves the Freudian peculiarly vulnerable to this coasting on his assumptions. His unusual advantage of method must be matched by an unusual susceptibility to the restless life of art if psychoanalysis is not to become a narcotic in his hands.

Chapter Five

STUDENT PROTEST AND ACADEMIC DISTANCE

In a book that deals with several "revolutionary" twistings of Freud, this review essay discusses the opposite and more common practice of invoking psychoanalytic notions to oppose change and demean its advocates. No one who remembers the academic year 1968–69, however, will imagine that I wrote this as an abstract exercise of perspective. Like many others who were caught between antiwar sentiment, concern for the besieged universities, and sympathy for excluded blacks, I was trying—with only partial success, I now see—to marshal ideas against a sense of helpless bewilderment.

*I*nnumerable essays and books on the university crisis, the generation gap, and the significance of the student left appear to have settled very little. Public anxiety has fastened upon these themes as a unitary threat or promise calling for a general position of resistance or welcome. Often the first casualty is logic. The distribution of power within universities is discussed as a conflict between strict and permissive rearing patterns, and tactical matters get confused with taking sides for or against a whole generation. No rhetorical strategies are spared to prove that we should or shouldn't allow ourselves to be guided by the superior idealism or utter depravity of the young.

No one who writes according to such formulas can be very helpful, but by far the worst record has been compiled by renowned liberals attempting to stave off the ideas of student radicals with improvised theories condemning or belittling them. Thus Louis Halle derives campus disorders from the currents of "nihilistic" thought (Freud, Lorenz, *et al.*) that have been delaying man's self-improvement for the past century or so. In his view "the student drive to destruction" is so patent that no evidence of it need be presented; the only problem is to decide which books and teachings are to blame. George Kennan adopts a tone of weepy *hauteur* as he contemplates the "defiant rags and hairdos" of "perverted and willful and stony-hearted youth." He too prefers to skip over the manifest disputes and get directly to the heart of the matter: bad taste, bad manners, lax upbringing, and want of respect for the Wilsonian concept of the university, "its air pure and wholesome with a breath of faith."

Jacques Barzun, after documenting many of the left charges against multiversities, suggests that student protest may spring from the teaching of misanthropic modern art. Student activists "are but acting out in life what their parents pay good money to see acted on the stage." Irving Howe proposes that "the very idea of commandment and regulation," after 150 years of skeptical assault, has finally dissolved and given way to "a psychology of unobstructed need." (So much for the "socialist" perspective.) And Diana Trilling, who sees her husband's university as a "white island, constantly shrinking" before "the meaner streets of the vicinity," declares that the flouting of parental authority these days is simply inexplicable: "does it not almost amount to a mutation in the species?" All would agree with Arthur Schlesinger, Jr., who does offer definite reasons for the activists' mood but finally insists that the struggle is being waged between "social process" on one hand and "anarchy" on the other.[1]

These efforts to drown the student movement in generalities deserve some explanation themselves. The announced aims of student radicals are threatening to many professors who are temperamentally loyal to that mixture of formalism, discretion, and indifference known as the academic process. Their personal niche needn't be directly jeopardized for them to feel perturbed by attacks against the more exposed parts of the university that are judged "irrelevant," or relevant to the wrong interests. Most academics are reconciled to the university's bending to dominant economic and political forces, so long as it is done inconspicuously. Precisely because campus upheavals bring these ties into the open, professors are inclined to react in a passionately euphemistic way. It is easier to speak of anarchy, nihilism, and the decline of civilization than to admit the compromised circumstances of one's professional life. The same point applies to critics outside the academy, for the student movement offends tacit notions of the benevolence of government, the dignity of commerce, and the delegation of authority which most people find essential to their mental peace. They respond as if the very principle of order, rather than specific privileged interests, were being menaced with extinction.

This reaction seems to be deeply ingrained in the mentality characterizing the greater part of American politics—a mentality derived from classic bourgeois liberalism as it has been modified by success. As C. Wright Mills noted, "Twentieth-century liberals have stressed ideals much more than theory or agency. But that is not all: they have stressed going agencies and institutions in such ways as to transform *them* into the foremost ideals of liberalism." [2] It is not surprising in this light that American academics, reluctant to admit that their universities are constantly evolving to accommodate money interests, tend to identify the institutional status quo with truth-seeking and tolerance: an attack on the standards undergirding elitist pluralism is taken as an attack on learning itself. Thus those who pound at the university's gates are judged according to whether or not they put their claims into the form of discourse already practiced on the inside. If not, they are "anarchists." When the crisis subsides and the institution has moved a modest step to left or right, the new arrangement will become the professorial norm for determining whether Western culture is about to receive its deathblow.

Lewis Feuer's ambitious and learned book on the strife between generations shows what can happen when this resistance of the academics is buttressed by a sweeping historical idea—in this case a potentially useful idea.[3] Feuer distinguishes student movements from ordinary college uprisings such as those led by the youthful Harlan Stone and Ronald Reagan. The latter have no serious political content and are adequately explained by the filial resentment and artificially prolonged dependency of college students. A genuine movement, taking on the aspect of a quasi-revolutionary assault on the political system, can only follow a significant "de-authoritization" of national leaders—loss of face through shameful policies or submission to an enemy power. But Feuer maintains that even such a movement will be driven by unconscious forces. Whatever their ideology, student movements will probably founder in ambivalence, excessive emotionalism, and ephemeral identifications with more truly oppressed groups. Feuer supports this assessment with much evidence culled from the past 150 years of world history. Yet the uses to which he puts his argument, particularly as he approaches his own time and place, finally become monotonous and absurd.

Feuer's most important mistake is to assume that irrational passion automatically makes for ineffective political behavior. Regardless of how despotic a regime may be, he invariably demands of its opponents that they "foster liberal democratic values." He shows no awareness that polite and patient reformism may be out of place in certain cases, or that survival may sometimes take precedence over decorum. Russians opposing the Czar, Chinese opposing the Kuomintang, Latin Americans with their curious "compulsion to discredit liberal democracy in the United States," and of course American students trying to exert group power are all deemed "irrational" because of their aggressive ways. Nowhere does Feuer indicate that the cultivation of decent personal values might be a separate matter from the choice of tactics for dealing with an enemy. The most durable liberal illusion is that violence never pays.

A related fantasy is that one's government never seeks domination over others, but is just kept busy protecting "freedom" around the globe; the liberal rule of thumb is self-interest for others' motives, altruism for ours. This attitude enters *The Conflict of Generations* as disbelief in the sincerity of anyone who questions American policies on any front. Feuer accuses one student, who had just returned from risking his life in the Mississippi Summer of 1964, of "hypocrisy" for wanting to lead the Berkeley Free Speech Movement; another's opposition

to the Vietnam war is described as a "pseudo-goal." The
American student movement turned from civil rights to Vietnam in early 1965, says Feuer, solely because the government's
success with civil rights legislation removed the generational
appeal of this issue; he neglects to mention the bombing of
North Vietnam. Without referring to the Bay of Pigs invasion
or to American policy at all, Feuer deduces that Fidel Castro's
Oedipus complex accounts for his anti-Americanism. And still
doing penance for his own student radicalism, he goes so far
as to hint that the McCarthy era never existed; it was "the
projected creation in large part of the bad conscience and cowardice of the radicals."

At the end of his b)ok Feuer observes that every dominant
generation as well as every student generation "has its projective unconscious, its inner resentments, its repressions and
exaggerations." The remark is tossed off as an afterthought, as
if it were not fundamentally relevant to his theme of "the
conflict of generations"; nowhere does he consider that it is
precisely the young who tend to be chosen as receptacles for
the envy and fear of their elders. A psychoanalytic outlook
such as Feuer professes should make him attentive to
voyeuristic and vindictive attitudes toward youth. As a psy-
chiatrist has recently said, reflecting on the brutality of American "correctional" facilities for the young, "It appears sometimes that our society needs its delinquents who act out
impulses which the adults do not or cannot and then requires
that the youth be viewed with indignation and censure." [4]

Feuer, however, detects the politics of the unconscious only
in student protesters, never in their antagonists. He tells us of
the New Left's "positive advocacy of promiscuity" and "positive advocacy of interracial sexuality," but says nothing about
the adult prurience that makes for censorship laws, harass-
ment of nonconforming youth, and fears of miscegenation. Indeed, the opinions of conservative adults seem altogether
beyond his criticism. "The fathers favor a policy of war in

Vietnam; therefore, the rebellious sons are for peace. The fathers criticize the Communists; therefore, the sons refuse to criticize the Communists." He actually goes so far as to diagnose the youthful tactic of "going limp" as masochism, comparable to "the submission of the intellectuals to the Stalinist terror." The passage is instructive not for what it says but for what it reveals about the fixated mentality of one generation of ex-radicals.

Feuer's interest in self-vindication shows through clearly in his chapter on the most controversial episode in his own career, the Berkeley Free Speech Movement. A critical moment of that year was the Academic Senate's defeat of the "Feuer Amendment," which sought to define a category of speech and advocacy that should not be tolerated on campus. Feuer's position was principled and arguable, though to most of us it seemed to invite unconstitutional prior restraint. But having undertaken to explain the debate, Feuer might at least be expected to summarize the arguments that decisively prevailed over his own. Instead, he caricatures them by misleadingly lifting a few odd-sounding phrases out of context and writing off the whole majority view as a product of anger, bewilderment, momentary exaltation, and servile desire to please the activist students. He would have us believe that his own emotional involvement in the FSM was merely the resigned melancholy of a social scientist observing that "the Law of Generational Struggle was in full ascendancy." Nothing could be less like the self-ironical spirit of psychoanalysis than this combination of infighting and sham transcendence.

Feuer's hypothesis for explaining student protest hinges on the concept of "de-authoritization": wherever a movement flourishes you can expect to find that generational hostility has been reinforced by contempt for a disgraced political regime. The hypothesis is useful because it anticipates the flareup of protest at seemingly unlikely spots and moments; a vacuum of true authority on the national level makes for a low boiling point everywhere. An obvious test of this idea is the past five years of American campus history, which Feuer does discuss. But his infatuation with the official policies of this period keeps him away from a clear judgment of whether and to what extent a de-authoritization has occurred. He grants the movement's existence but implies, contrary to his own formula, that the very stability of the American order has been the chief source of resentment.

Once we get away from Feuer's personal bias it is not difficult to see that a limited but genuine de-authoritization has catalyzed student protest in this decade. Two new books, William M. Birenbaum's *Overlive* and Immanuel Wallerstein's *University in Turmoil*, fill in much of what Feuer has neglected to say.[5] Starting with different emphases—Wallerstein's on the international political situation, Birenbaum's on what urban universities have been doing to their ghetto surroundings— these books reach similar conclusions. Both writers understand that widespread and vehement protest must derive from real circumstances and from a diffuse uneasiness with the government's broken promises. Both take for granted, as Feuer does not, that universities are instruments of an economic system and as such are logical pressure points for dissidents who want either to change the system or to gain entrance to it.

These books taken together indicate two broad ways in which America has been losing the respect of some of its most sensitive college students. First, the attempted relaxation of the Cold War in the sixties has had the effect of discrediting the previous decade's pieties. People with no economic or mental stake in "defense" have begun to feel that the sword-rattling, the spy network, the frenzy over left-wing influences, and the indefinite postponement of domestic justice for the poor and black have been unnecessary, or necessary only to those who sought to extend American militarism. Yet the policies continue after their supposed rationale has become incredible. Disenchantment turns to rage when the shopworn fears of world conquest are trotted out to justify the mass slaughter of Vietnamese partisans. Some young Americans have been gagging on the "free world" propaganda that nearly everyone was swallowing a few years ago.

Secondly, universities since World War II have increasingly merged their purposes and style with the government's. Both have become more bureaucratic and anonymous, more responsive to the largest corporations, and more concerned with counterrevolutionary technology and ideology, all the while making well-publicized but token gestures of democratization. As property owners and employers the universities have mirrored the opportunism and discrimination of the society at large. Politically conscious students of the sixties have started to learn, outside the classroom of course, that the contemplative academic haven has been a primary contributor to the warfare state. Again, the shock has been considerable precisely because the older view was such an article of general faith.

This summary places more reliance than Feuer would on the manifest content of student rhetoric, but it is consistent with his approach. By comparison with his fullest modern examples—Russian protest before the Revolution, French and German between the World Wars—a modest de-authoritization has touched off a modest-sized movement. Whether the conditions of student life have worsened is doubtful, but amenities do not appease a feeling of revulsion. If anything, they exacerbate it. Consider the opening sentence of Tom Hayden's prescient Port Huron Statement of 1962: "We are people of this generation, bred in at least modest comfort, housed now in universities, looking uncomfortably to the world we inherit." The question has not been how to gain one's withheld rights but whether to accept one's legacy—a moral or spiritual problem rather than a practical one.

For this reason Feuer's psychosocial method of explanation remains useful, irrespective of his prejudices. Students often engage in what Feuer calls "projective" politics, as opposed to the relative realism and materialism of class and ethnic groups. They seek out symbolic issues distant from their immediate situation in order to express or resolve ambivalence about authority and identity. Among students a kind of claustrophobia at the thought of membership in a too pervasive, too predictable, and too discriminatory order gets translated into fraternal and ascetic identification with those who are exempt from any charge of being its heirs: the black proletariat, migrant farm workers, NLF peasants. And this identification requires a mistaken perception of political realities or even a provocation of repressive malice from authorities.

There is indeed some truth to the charge that one segment of the American student left has invited the crackdown which it takes to be the very essence of the liberal regime. This is often defended as a way of polarizing the uncommitted, but of course the uncommitted have largely ended up at the wrong pole—and yet the tactics remain unchanged. One must conclude that for some radicals the spectacle of students being beaten and gassed carries a perverse satisfaction of its own, a revelation that the "fascist police state" so long anticipated has surfaced in all its horror. The irresponsibility of such thinking consists largely in its obscuring the real preconditions for fascism that do exist in America today: an economy that can no longer yield an adequate profit rate without a high degree of state control, monopolistic practices, domination of client states, and a perpetual war scare, plus a widespread willingness in the working class to blame an ethnic and political minority for the system's troubles. The police are a significant part of this restless class, but they are not fascism incarnate. To treat them as such is to redouble their hostility and to squander valuable energy.

Feuer's concept of "projective politics" is suggestive enough to raise once again many of the challenges that have been hurled at the New Left by its Establishment foes. We can set aside Louis Halle's and Jacques Barzun's supercilious explanations of protest, but the doubts about effectiveness voiced by such serious critics as Nathan Glazer are another matter.[6] Can a movement with no program be counted on to achieve a better society, or indeed to achieve anything besides temporary inconveniences to those who have power and know how to consolidate it? Are the students capable of sustaining discipline and taking politically necessary steps that are not reinforced by generational animus—for instance, cooperating with the blue collar and clerical classes who are theoretically detachable from the corporate elite but happen to despise radical students? How much devotion to democratic ideals is implied by a movement that chafes under "repressive tolerance" and regularly uses minority coercion in the name of "the people"? How radical are those students who invite cancellation of the university forum for radical analysis by harassing and intimidating their ideological foes?

These are nasty questions, the asking of which is usually taken as exposing one's conservatism. The standard left reply is that the students are feeling their way toward an unimagined better world and that their horror of war and racism is a guarantee of reliable intentions. This is a tempting but not a logical line of argument, and ultimately it amounts to an abdication of personal commitment. Following the movement, "getting over one's violence hangup," replaces the drab business of assessing the actual strength of radical forces and the possibilities for making inroads into a conservative and relatively stable society.

Romantic revolutionism has never made a revolution anywhere. Marx distrusted militant students, Engels regarded them as mischievous "officer candidates without an army," and Lenin came reluctantly to see the student desperadoes of pre-1917 Russia as incurably bourgeois. The historical record is littered with abortive student movements that betrayed their announced ends, acted with suicidal impulsiveness, and veered wildly between authoritarianism and apathy. The American movement is too fragmentary and new to permit of any definite judgment of its ethics or its power, but under the present counterattack it is already having a crisis of morale. To be "for the students" in a reflex way isn't a service either to radicalism or to the students as people.

But to ask whether student rebels can overcome their debilities is to misconstrue the issue, for the movement's success depends precisely on its ceasing to be exclusively a student matter. The unmasking of questionable purposes in official America is more important than any calculation of how much is won or lost in the sum of campus showdowns. The movement finally amounts to an ongoing critique of the managerial, aggressively evangelistic mentality on which the current American dispensation rests; whoever abandons this mentality carries the movement within himself, whether or not he approves of student tactics and leaders. The hope and strength of radicalism lies not in its gaining formal concessions but in its redirecting inhibited energies toward humanistic ends. It isn't necessary to imagine an economic collapse or a concerted revolt against the American empire to arrive at a different idea of the future than, say, Zbigniew Brzezinski's "technetronic society," which is only an extrapolation from the present convergence of technology and centralized power. An entire way of life that depends on paranoid fictions and bureaucratic anonymity can be discredited by its inability to contain what it has repressed.

The university remains vital to this debunking process, not only because it allows critical thought to flourish but also because it is a peculiarly visible arena of competition for social rewards. Whatever the society cannot amicably settle will be dramatized and aggravated there. This is a point which radical activists, for all their "projective politics," have understood more soberly than their elders. In the current academic year they have subordinated themselves to what might superficially seem a conformist effort—the struggle of young black men and women to gain a foothold in the system which has kept them down. In fact, this struggle is nothing less than revolutionary. Black students are not settling for what Nathan Hare of San Francisco State calls super-tokenism, the majority's "plucking many of the most promising members from a group while failing to alter the lot of the group as a whole." [7] They want nothing less than the elevation of their people *as* a people, and to this end they have necessarily become trenchant critics of everything that white America has hidden. They are bringing to the academy that "voracious taste for the concrete" which Fanon finds typical of the ex-colonized, and which makes further mystification impossible.

Ironically, this undertaking is greeted with fear and anxiety by many radical professors, perhaps because it is taking place on their own territory. There is a difference between sympathizing with Venezuelan guerrillas and being personally confronted with "non-negotiable demands," beatings, and arson. But more than squeamishness or self-protection is involved; a radical scholar who believes in the university's long-range utility for social renovation cannot be happy with tactics and stated aims that seem to threaten intellectual freedom. The discreetly political university defined by Kerr and Barzun allows some excellent radical scholarship to survive on the grounds that it is truthful; but the open, compensatory politicization advocated by Nathan Hare seems ominous. The subordination of inquiry to what Hare calls "Black ego development," the imposition of tests for blackness and radicalism in the choice of faculty, and the creation of ideologically satisfying counter-disciplines to refute "white" history, sociology, etc., all smack of thought control. No wonder, then, that radical professors are finding themselves torn between their sense of historic necessity and their feelings as academics.

These contradictions cannot be escaped. They can be understood, however, as transitional for both the university and the society. If America absorbs the sweeping democratization being proposed, current militant tactics will obviously become unnecessary; if it cannot, questions of academic style may be preempted by a social explosion. It is pointless to ask people now on the bottom, awakening to their latent power, to respect the intellectual luxuries enjoyed by those near the top. The way to defend scholarly objectivity may be to refrain from using it as a screening device to blindly exclude the "unqualified." If the university exists to offer conditions for learning to people who have decided that higher education would be useful to them, it will have to reshape itself to accommodate those it has never cared to understand. The main stumbling block, the real enemy, is not the probably transitory "black anti-intellectualism" but the elitism that purports to find this so incomprehensible and uses it as a pretext for automatic rejection of black demands.

The unique strength of the black student movement, as opposed to all the movements dissected by Feuer, is its claim on the conscience of the white majority. Its dynamic is such that black liberation and white awareness come to the same thing; the overrated phenomenon of "backlash" recedes as lifelong unconscious lies are correctly named and exposed. This is why a tiny group of black students in a college far removed from the ghetto can get results undreamt-of by SDS. And the lesson continues after the confrontation is over. The very necessity for ethnic enclaves within the citadel of white individualism is a rebuke to the system's pretense of democracy; what Hare calls "the programmed educational maladjustment of the Black race" can only be remedied by a racial solidarity which shocks and embarrasses—and thus enlightens—those who have never thought clearly about exploitation. As Eldridge Cleaver has said:

> For all these years whites have been taught to believe in the myth they preached, while Negroes have had to face the bitter reality

of what America practiced. But without the lies and distortions, white Americans would not have been able to do the things they have done. When whites are forced to look honestly upon the objective proof of their deeds, the cement of mendacity holding white society together swiftly disintegrates. On the other hand, the core of the black world's vision remains intact, and in fact begins to expand and spread into the psychological territory vacated by the non-viable white lies, i.e., into the minds of young whites.[8]

What the young whites are learning is not simply the privileged position they have held, but also the subtle deprivation accompanying it. To be locked unknowingly into a mentality which has to negate and prettify and rationalize is to be out of touch with oneself. The blacks' insistence on connecting identity to learning and learning to committed action is thus of great potential significance to all students in all disciplines of the self-estranged knowledge industry. The answer to student alienation is not, as Lewis Feuer would have it, a "purified idealism" based on forswearing generational "demonry," but a humanizing of the educational process and of the society itself. There is nothing fortuitous in the fact that the main hope for this development lies with those who understand the duplicity of corporate America without having to open a book. Coming to full self-consciousness now, they are starting to teach the rest of us what they have always known.

Chapter Six

DO LITERARY STUDIES
HAVE AN IDEOLOGY?

This talk, presented to a forum of the Modern Language Association in 1969, was widely misinterpreted at the time as a New Left manifesto. In fact it was an effort to speak independently of both the MLA regulars, who seemed to me to care too little about stopping the Vietnam war, and the activists who had recently shaken the organization. If my tone here is sometimes taunting, my aim is the traditionally scholarly one of trying to combat intellectual prejudice.

The passing of American capitalism into an anxious phase has, I think, made some of the ideas in this talk more accessible than they once were. Now that the economic empire has dwindled, its former power is readily, even nostalgically, admitted. But confused loyalties on my own part also allowed some vulnerable simplifications to enter these pages. The concluding suggestion, for example, that literary criticism should and would focus increasingly on factors lying behind literature now strikes me as a questionable private effort to align my Freudian interests with radical purpose. Literary criticism, to my subsequent relief, neglected to obey my call.

Our common task this afternoon is, I suppose, to define what literary education should be and explain why the real thing differs so markedly from the ideal; to inquire whether scholarship, in its present condition, shall be suffered to live; to characterize the emerging social crisis in America and decide who caused it; to take a stand on student violence and institutional violence; to decide whether it is all right to use the term "academic freedom" without a sneer; to determine a teacher's political responsibility to his students; and of course to judge whether the MLA is more to be pitied than censured, or vice versa. Fortunately, two whole hours have been set aside for this inquiry. My title, however, is meant to convey a hope that some of the burden will fall on other speakers; I only intend to provoke some thought about the possibility that our literary studies have been significantly affected by an ideological bias.

The temptation to self-righteousness on this issue is strong, and after a few precautionary paragraphs I am going to succumb to it. Our debate today will be pointless, however, unless we keep in mind the plight we share as well as the differences that make us distrust and accuse one another. Trading slogans of "repressive tolerance" and "irrelevance" on one side with "scholarly neutrality" and "professionalism" on the other will gain us nothing beyond a superfluous confirmation that "they," the ones with the wrong shibboleths, are a menace to learning.

Our real situation is more ironical than such Manichean gestures would suggest. Those among us who grumble about repressive tolerance are exercising it as they complain, and would pine for it again if it were supplanted by repression pure and simple. Those who uphold the neutrality of the academy scarcely seem to have noticed that most of this neutrality has been bought out over the past twenty-five years, so that the ideal they are defending is just that—an ideal, not a fact. Cold War America seems to have played a joke on all of us. Whether we have tigerish dreams of revolution or pastoral yearnings for the vanished academic cloister, we all inhabit a mixed world, as comfortable as it is corrupt. Perhaps because America is still very much a Protestant country, what we have most in common seems to be our unwillingness to accept this compromised reality and work within it knowingly. We can be fairly well divided into people who disclaim any taint of the system's abominations (meanwhile punctually collecting salary checks) and people who see nothing amiss that a little discipline and conventional study couldn't rectify. The latter group is, of course, less puritanical, but this is only what you would expect from the anti-revolutionary faction in any dispute.

I happen to have affinities with both groups, one by background and one by the recent trauma of the Vietnam war, which has made me attentive to arguments about the long-range tendencies of the American system. Once those tendencies are even dimly understood, and one has grasped the almost total acquiescence of the universities in the expansionist schemes of business and government, it becomes hard to retain a moderate argumentative style. One feels like shouting at one's fellow professors, begging them to drop the scales from their eyes and see what one has only lately seen oneself: the perversion of scholarly research to purposes of exploitation and conquest, and the more pervasive influence of a socially manipulative style of thinking on the evolution of various academic fields. One is awestruck by the unimpaired capacity of scholars to sermonize about the value-free university when their daily walk from parking lot to office may take them past guarded institutes where the best-paid of their colleagues are learning how ten cities can be destroyed by one missile, how botulism can be suspended in an aerosol spray, or how a whole peasantry can be bombed and starved off its land and into relocation camps. One suspects a disingenuousness in literary intellectuals who choose not to comprehend what they could read in their morning newspaper.

But such cynicism is inappropriate. I think it can be assumed that all of us are primarily concerned with truth, not power, and that we cherish our mental independence. Though it would be worthwhile to look into the effect of agencies like the CIA and USIA on literary studies, I am sure one would find nothing comparable either in magnitude or serviceability to, say, Project Camelot or the Michigan State field trip to arm Ngo Dien Diem against his own citizenry. Our normal enterprises, after all, seem well outside the most urgent pragmatic interests of the state; as C. Wright Mills once said, there can be no sellout where there is nothing to be sold. The famous ratio for successful counter-insurgency, ten anthropologists for each guerrilla, has no literary equivalent. What bears investigating is our remarkable political innocence rather than our guilt.

Even those of us who take up the government's invitation to lecture abroad about the spiritual strivings of Cooper and Sims while napalm and phosphorus continue to rain on Vietnamese villages would deny any imputation of compromised principles, and they would be right. The whole field of American Literature and American Studies is taciturn about such themes as racism, imperialism, and monopoly, but eloquent about myths, motifs, and morals—the Fulbrighter's stock-in-trade. Given this situation, it would be absurd to maintain that the government had subverted a few men's minds by dangling some opportunities for fun and travel. We are dealing rather with a congruency between ideologically useful attitudes and what scholars already believe, and the question to be asked is whether ideology has helped to shape those beliefs without the scholars' conscious awareness. This would be a relatively undramatic but quite serious politicization of learning, for someone who does not even know that he is thinking propagandistically is farther from objectivity than one who decides to suppress his real views.

I believe that our literary studies generally do have an ideological cast, less in what they say than in what they refuse to consider. Plausible lines of investigation that might lead to disquieting conclusions, or that would employ politically alien categories of thought, are not pursued, while dubious but politically reinforced assumptions are elevated into articles of faith. There is no way of proving absolutely that these irrationalities must be explained as the result of an unconscious ideological consensus, but one can observe that the same biases characterize the social sciences, whose answerability to the current political order is undeniable.

I hope I needn't insist that we are living under a capitalistic set of arrangements, and that our regnant ideology is therefore bound to be a capitalist one. Capitalism is a system operated by and for large investors, and when it runs into trouble, the state, which is answerable to those same investors, intervenes to safeguard their profits regardless of the social cost. I cannot pause to defend this proposition, but it is consistent with all known evidence, and it is particularly appropriate to the present period, when the government has propped the domestic economy with enormous subsidies to the corporate rich, mostly under the pretext of national defense. The ideology surrounding this inverted welfarism is no less capitalistic than Jeremy Bentham's belief in free trade. When capitalism moves from underdevelopment to overdevelopment, from acquiring basic industries within a home nation to imposing an international order in which the desired flow of raw materials and sales is encouraged by armed force, an advanced school of thought arises favoring state regulation, foreign aid, placation of the unemployed, and similar measures to help things go smoothly. Thus, for example, Nelson Rockefeller is as much a capitalist ideologue as Barry Goldwater; being a Rockefeller, he just happens to have a broader understanding of the system's needs.

Though it may be bad taste to say so, capitalism rests on exploitation and social inequality; these are not its casual by-products but in large part its raison d'être. The main task of capitalist ideology is to disguise this fact, whether through the fantasy of steady social progress or that of equal opportunity or that of saving the world from all sorts of evils, from pestilence and paganism through Bolshevism. The deception, however, is usually not Machiavellian but sentimental: those who acquiesce in the order want to believe that it has a human face, and to a limited extent they succeed in lending it one.

This is especially true of academics, who are mostly decent, tolerant, socially conscious people with an obsessive scrupulosity about the correctness of their words and deeds. Scholars are grateful for the genuine intellectual freedom they enjoy under capitalism in its confident periods, and they would like to think that this freedom is guaranteed by the general commitment to constitutional ideals. Some scholars have, in addition, a special patriotism based on their self-image as public advisers who will lead the ignorant politicians into enlightened paths, but many others are temperate and unquestioning for a humbler reason: they see themselves as economically unproductive, easily dispensable drones who could be tossed out of their universities into the distasteful commercial world. For whatever reason, fundamental critical perceptions tend to be muted or diverted into a reformist vein. In any crisis, foreign or domestic or intramural, the typical scholar can be counted on to welcome a speedy restoration of order and routine, no matter who is in the right.

This is to say that most scholars are liberals, and that liberalism, for all its amiable intentions and good works, is somewhat handicapped for political understanding. Liberalism takes the most recent phase of capitalism to be reality itself in all its mysterious complexity, and then improvises ad hominem explanations for whatever social dysfunctions it perceives. (Conservatism, not minding the dysfunctions so long as the profits are coming in, goes through fewer mental gymnastics and has a simpler, sterner vision.) The morally overwrought quality of much liberal thinking derives, I believe, not merely from indignation but from the strain of trying not to perceive that capitalism's logical tendency is to preserve inequality, deplete resources, pollute the elements, keep an underclass out of work, and tyrannize over the economies of other nations. The attempt to address such problems without calling attention to property relations yields a confused, symbolic, and hortatory thinking which seizes on immediate occasions for outrage or sympathy while neglecting structural factors. Each new military intervention, if not quickly and successfully concluded, is a tragic blunder that "we" can never make again, for "we" have learned better—as if it had been our decision in the first place. Each new welfare program is an all-out war on injustice, definitive proof that "we care." Each new articulate candidate with good manners and a patrician distaste for politics will surely save our country from its real internal enemies, the uncouth rednecks and crazy generals who lack all humor and compassion.

Inevitably, a social scientist who holds these shallow expectations in private life will carry them into his academic studies. American social science is united in its lack of serious interest in American power. It willingly follows what Martin Nicolaus has called "the one and only general sociological law that has ever been discovered, namely that the oppressors research the oppressed." [1] Thus, though the U.S. has an overseas network for more than 3,000 military bases, a formidable array of client states, and direct foreign investments of over $60 billion—in effect the world's third largest economy—this

major force in the contemporary world is not considered a
proper subject of academic study, and there is not a single
funded research project looking into it.[2] That we have positively stunted the development of some of the world's most
abused countries, extracting their minerals, bribing and arm-
ing their feudal oligarchies, and preventing the economic di-
versification that might make them independent of us, is apparently unknown not only to a specialist in development like
Walt Rostow, but also to a more authentic liberal like John
Kenneth Galbraith, whose urbane 418-page apology for monopoly, *The New Industrial State*, gives no hint that our corporations do any business abroad at all.[3] Naturally, then, there
can be no study of how the government takes military steps to
protect and expand the forgotten investments. On the contrary: by restricting his attention only to that part of the order
that is already monopolized while ignoring its more classical
rapaciousness elsewhere, Galbraith is able to compose a veri-
table ode to the giant post-competitive corporation, only re-
minding us that "we" must keep trying to improve our cultural tone.

When a whole academic field such as economics refuses to
set up any perspective outside our own Keynesian order and
devotes its major energies not to understanding the economy's
history and consequences but to tinkering with its seemingly
eternal "business cycles" so as to prevent catastrophe, not
much can be expected by way of value-neutral objectivity. The
very categories of accepted economic thinking, such as gross
national product, aggregate demand, and structural unemploy-
ment, assume the profit values of capitalism as objectively
given, and help to reconcile us uncritically to the government's
preference for socially wasteful over socially useful spending
and to the forced idleness of large numbers of people. Similarly, a political science that dwells fondly on polls and elec-
tions without considering new centers of unreviewable power;
a sociology that studies belief systems and attitude disposi-

tions apart from historical process; an anthropology that examines "natives" in the wake of colonial conquest but shows no interest either in colonialism or in the culture of the putatively neutral investigators; and a psychology that imprisons and debases its objects of study while counseling businessmen and advertisers on the most efficient means of inducing compliant behavior—all have been appreciably shaped by a single ideology. The requirements and predilections of the ruling order are not only left unexamined, they are casually accepted as guidelines for the choice of projects, methods, and assumptions.

Capitalist scholarship that deals with the contemporary world is distinguished by its mistaking of an ideological consensus for neutrality, its reluctance to question capitalism itself, its preference for short views and abstracted statistics over dynamic historical understanding, its embarrassment about recognizing power, and its penchant for isolating phenomena from their structural causes. On the last of these points, one is reminded of Marx's and Engels' critique of Hegel, who had elevated ideas to a state of autonomy, mystifying their origin in the defense of specific property arrangements and treating them as the principal agents of history. American social science is impatient with ideas, preferring easily disposable constructs such as opinion samples, voting patterns, and consumer preferences, but it treats these trivialities as if they conveyed the broadest truth, and in so doing it obscures class dominance. The proliferation of bland, narrowly defined research acts as a filibuster against questions about the order as a whole, while each gainfully employed scholar comforts himself with the thought that he is adding a grain to the gross world product of objective knowledge.

For several reasons, this relatively clear picture of ideologically influenced study becomes clouded when we turn to literary criticism and scholarship. Rational understanding is not the sole aim of our discipline, and for many of us it is a poor second to the cultivation of taste. Flagrant departures from rationality are more easily indulged in our field, and one is never sure whether a given instance should be laid to political prejudice, emotive fervor, or sheer preciosity. The fact that our work generally avoids discussion of capitalism is not much of a scandal, though capitalism is reflected in most of the literature we study. The escape clause is that we conceive our task to be the study of end products rather than of raw social forces. Even historians, who resemble us in some of their conventional thought patterns, are worse off in this respect, for they are often expected to come up with explanatory formulations. By contrast, we try to establish rapport with certain objects *as* objects, and some of our weightiest theorists even argue that we have no business explaining anything, for explanation would diminish our respect for art. Though it is only a short step from this state of mind to the virgin anti-intellectualism of our freshmen who regard all discourse as a profanation of selfhood, we believe our lack of curiosity to be more sophisticated and high-principled than theirs.

As soon as we look a little more closely at the imperative to prostrate ourselves before literature's autonomous emanations of meaning, we begin to see that here, too, ideology has been at work. It can hardly be coincidental that in socialist countries an exactly opposite attitude prevails. A revolutionary society or one that still feels its existence imperiled by class enemies finds the meaning of literary works in the social dynamics they express or promote. To be sure, officially sanctioned socialist criticism is almost always simpleminded and venal, like any other mental effort that must flatter a bureaucracy and meet a doctrinal test; our criticism seems to do better if only because it is less closely supervised. Yet the root assumption that literature conveys class meaning is, as a Georg Lukács can show, both true and important. A criticism neglecting the historical struggles behind art's genesis and stressing the formal harmonies, resolved differences, and sententious wisdom that emerge at the other end of artistic process is well suited to a prosperous and entrenched society. Such a criticism is certainly less ideological than one that makes political correctness the touchstone of aesthetic value, but it does have an ideological aspect in its very neglect of social forces. It rests upon, and helps to foster, the illusion of present classlessness—an illusion whose effective function is to ensure compliance with disguised class governance.

Capitalism in general seems to promote a style of humanistic discourse that errs on the side of vagueness and false transcendence rather than on that of dogmatic simplicity; there is little need for militant moralism when one is reaping the profits of an imperial order. But capitalism is by nature unstable; not only does it expand absolutely over time, it suffers periodic convulsions which shake the faith of intelligent people. Americans today are still living in the aftermath of capitalism's worst crash so far, which was ended not by the negligible efforts of the New Deal but by the industrial spurt of World War II, which has been artificially prolonged through a militarization of the peacetime economy. Whether this militarization can be stemmed is a matter of dispute; meanwhile, "defense" has poisoned our lives in many ways,[4] not least in its heightening of the dissociated mentality normally required for self-respect under capitalism. While most intellectuals are resistant to Cold War paranoia, we find other, equally timely, ways of channeling anxiety about the destructive and insecure basis of our "security."

American literary criticism has many conflicting strands, but over several decades one can make out approximate shifts in spirit that correspond to the vicissitudes of the economy. No one would dispute that the thirties were a time of ideological debate among critics and that from the forties until very recently that debate has seemed increasingly quaint and embarrassing. Many of us, like our social science colleagues, have been ready to believe that the end of ideology has arrived and

that the leftist squabbles of the past were pointless and imma-
ture. Those squabbles were indeed strident, and the current
revival of their excommunicative hairsplitting gives one cause
to doubt that history teaches anything at all. Yet it could be
argued that the very best American discussions of literature
were generated by the political ferment preceding World War
II. Critics like Wilson, Trilling, Burke, Kazin, and Howe had to
ask themselves where ideology ended and art began. Their
urgently personal efforts to accommodate their sense of aesthetic complexity to their politics, which seemed to be falling in
ruins at the end of the thirties, yielded apprehensions of literature that were full of a clarifying passion. One need not agree
with the accommodations themselves in order to grant the importance of the effort and the excitement it generated for others. When we compare such criticism with the formalism and
static didacticism that have characterized much of the inter-
vening period, we may wonder whether a certain political
anguish may not be essential to good criticism. Perhaps our
most challenging criticism is more indebted to the Depression
and the shock of Stalinism than to the theoretical efforts of
Eliot and Richards.

It is widely acknowledged that much recent criticism has
been characterized by a primness of tone, a spirit of dry routine, and a preoccupation with abstracted formal patterns. The
New Critics, with their generally nostalgic politics and their
ostentatious piety, are usually blamed for this arid development, but the accusation is unfair, for most of the men who
have been called New Critics were artists and thinkers with a
clear sense of their commitments. The hallmark of most criticism produced today is precisely its low degree of commitment, its air of occupying a niche rather than of claiming some
territory. The niche is the one where most of us reside—the af-
fluent and multifarious university, the crowning ornament of a
credit-card civilization whose basis cannot be examined with a

clear conscience. Our obvious difference from the liveliest critics of thirty years ago is that we are completely at home in academe. And if the most general trait of recent criticism is its absence of worry over what the business and loyalty of the critic should be, this is because the answer is intuitively known: he should enter the academic hierarchy and do whatever it asks of him.

A history of postwar criticism might begin by setting aside the various contending factions and examining the university itself, with its haven for both upward mobility and snobbery, its trials and perquisites and sinecures—in short, its capacity to become a substitute world. With tenure for wafer and the assistant professorship for circumcision, nothing further is needed to account for the submissive and ritualistic aspect of most published work. Perhaps the most eloquent fact about contemporary schools of criticism is how alike they sound. All of them, even those that affect familiarity with terrible dionysian powers, have a cautious politeness and orderliness, an air of going through predetermined motions. Even the more original spirits seem loyal to the temper of the times. One notices, for example, that young critics are now likely to invent an entire terminological system with which to overwhelm a single text, and one is startled at such a squandering of ingenuity. Reflecting, however, that conventional methods have pretty much picked over the modest harvest of English and American literature, one can grasp the need for novelty. Constant revolution in the means of promotion is now the emergent law.

Yet even insincerity expresses certain values, and predictably enough, recent criticism usually expresses the values of capitalism in its monopoly phase. Not justice and passion, but order and sophistication are implicitly treasured. The critic's relation to his text is manipulative rather than involved. Instead of accepting and examining the temperamental affinity that led him to treat a certain author, he displays his capacity to perform correct and efficient operations that will give him total possession of the work. Writers who may have been scarcely able to contain their sensuality or savage indignation are thus transmuted into masters of cunning who have subliminally engineered our responses. Their seeming disunities are secret unities after all—indeed, are devices to trip us up.[5] And if it is often hard for us to accept such a depiction of the writer, we at least know that the critic has succeeded in replacing *his* vulnerable feelings with cold and subtle strategy. It is like the computerized pacification of a province.

In the oddly segregated portion of our field known as "scholarship," things have changed much less over the past four decades than one could gather from following the "critics." For most literary scholars there has been no end of ideology because there was never any ideology in the first place; as in the social sciences, a posture of neutrality before facts has obviated questions of political value. Yet this very unconcern has ensured a hospitality to the assumptions ingrained in our system, and in some cases those assumptions can be blamed for shallow thinking about literature. It is, for instance, an absence of feeling for historical dynamics that allows some scholars to account for one author's work merely by the "influence" of another's, as if his life situation did not contain features that readied him for one sort of guidance. Much history-of-ideas scholarship commits the same error; it is Hegel's error of taking the verbal precipitates of power relations to be power itself, so that material circumstances can be altogether discounted. Or again, note the political up-to-dateness of commentaries that mistake an era's dominant value system for its whole play of social forces. If "the Renaissance" believed in holy kingship or the Great Chain of Being, the problem of any single case has been settled in advance. The scholar, occupying a post in an institution whose purposes and values are by now sensitively attuned to those of the state, perhaps even having sworn his ideological loyalty on pain of firing and blacklisting, is undisposed to imagine that a writer might have questioned the myths by whose means the ruling families stayed in power.

If we can discern such a thing as capitalist scholarship and begin to see its blind spots, this is possible only because capitalism itself is once again in trouble. The suffocation of dialogue under present-day socialism might suggest that the very chaos of capitalism, cruel and dangerous though it is, is the best guarantee of intellectual ferment. But such reasoning forgets that capitalism favors democratic procedures only to the extent that they enhance trade; there are no known instances in which values of free inquiry have won out over the imperatives of profit when profit has decided to cast its lot with totalitarianism. The increasing centralization of American power, policy, and communications, the persecution of dissidents, and the forceful maintaining of imperial outposts ought to inspire some scholarly caution about investing faith in modern capitalism's libertarian avowals.

For the moment, however, the strains that became visible in the 1960's have begun to yield a fundamental debate about intellectual values and methods. While the challenges to obscurantist scholarship are sometimes uninformed and even anti-intellectual, it is becoming possible in several fields, including literary study, to perceive that the old legitimations for conventional work—objectivity, neutrality, humanistic values, "culture"—are not what they once seemed. Whereas many critics of thirty years ago were prompted by political disillusion to seek a truer order within art, I suspect that the best critics in the immediate future will reject such escapism and demand that works be understood, not as transcendent icons and refuges from the world, but as contingent, imperfect expressions of social and mental forces. Without necessarily having any political end in view, such an understanding will have political determinants and political effects, for it will share in the awakening from Cold-War mystification. I would like to think that this awakening will be welcomed by everyone who respects scholarship's ideal of shedding prejudice and discovering principles that make the world accessible to reason.

Chapter Seven

OFFING CULTURE: LITERARY STUDY AND THE MOVEMENT

This essay was written as an exploration of differences with onetime allies whose interest in mere peace had all but vanished by 1970–71. Today the Movement itself has vanished, but the issues it dramatized still bear discussing.

Although I didn't address Freudian criticism in this essay, the reviewing of one blatant kind of reductionism did force me to think more skeptically than before about closed interpretive systems in general. In this sense the present chapter and the two that follow it make a consistent series.

> *"To ignore the fact that each thing has a character
> of its own and not what we wish to demand of it is
> in my opinion the real capital sin . . ."*
> Ortega y Gasset

*E*veryone knows that the study of literature, along with the universities that harbor it, is suffering a protracted crisis of confidence. It is now common for professors to announce that they can't understand why they have spent decades in the library when life is so much more interesting than books, or when the draft has made a mockery of the academic cloister, or when the old should be learning from the young. The familiar genteel claims for literary study as fostering an aristocracy of taste and sophistication no longer sound plausible after the student revolts of the later sixties, and no other claims have filled their place. Yet most professors feel uneasy with the main line of attack that has been launched against their field. They wonder whether the charges of "irrelevance," "sellout," and "brainwashing" have been triggered by misdeeds of theirs or by a general cultural eruption that happened to intersect their sleepy outpost of knowledge.

Those of us who have been most appalled and angered by the Vietnam war have tended to shy away from this question and, if anything, to add our own complaints to those of activists. The New Left, which was or seemed to be the most courageous faction of peace, has also been the main source of anti-academic sentiment, and it did succeed in linking the universities to the war machine. For a while the revelations of hypocrisy and complicity were impressive enough to put in abeyance whatever doubts we may have felt about the Movement's own nature and purpose. Even though literary study looked to be one of the fields least worth corrupting for official ends, and even though a turn toward "relevance" never seemed quite the right prescription, we shared the Movement's sense that something was drastically missing.

Now, however, the New Left has lost much of its impetus and credibility. "What was once good propaganda," according to Andrew Kopkind, "became bad rhetoric," and as the Movement failed to adapt to a changing situation it "began visibly to disintegrate." [1] The New Left now looks less like a force for rational analysis than a breakthrough of feeling, a mobilization of guilt and penance. If so, then the shortcomings of literary study have to be considered apart from the activist perspective. Yet not entirely apart, for the cultural strain that produced the New Left is also felt by critics and teachers of literature. To grasp the New Left's meaning as a cultural enterprise is also to reopen the question of whether literary study deserves to survive, for the New Left has been, all along, an embodied rejection of the assumptions of academic humanism.

By the Movement or the New Left I refer to the amorphous group of mostly youthful, white, middle-class Americans who developed solidarity around the issues of civil rights (and later black power), war protest, and the rights of students, and who exhibit a suspicion of formal ideology, a belief in mass-participatory, confrontational action, a disdain for consumerism and for liberal institutions, and a feeling of brotherhood with foreign and domestic victims of capitalism. [2] Although they regard themselves as revolutionaries, their politics are for the most part a series of improvisations in response to outrages. From the very beginning, even before Tom Hayden's Port Huron Statement of 1962, the Movement has insisted on *feeling* its way toward an appropriate style, and different factions have been at odds with regard to violence or nonviolence, single-issue or global-issue orientation, opposition to the Cold War university or to rational knowledge in general. As a result, it is hard to discern "the Movement position" on any topic. It may nevertheless be possible to isolate a core of

Movement sentiment that has survived all the mergers, defections, and contradictions of a decade's experience, and which manifests itself quite distinctly when cultural and literary matters are debated.

The pivotal question for anyone attempting to characterize the New Left is whether it began as an upwelling of revulsion against unusual episodes of war and racism or as an expression of the anxieties and unmet needs of young people in a time of prosperity. Those who share the Movement's moral passion automatically favor the first view, while conservatives and disillusioned liberals take the latter, often explaining away objective grievances in the process. Now, in the Movement's evident decline, we can perhaps accept the "conservative" case without the politics that accompanied it.

The Movement's campaign against segregation began after the Supreme Court had undertaken the most dramatic gain for civil rights since Emancipation, and in those days the Vietnam war was of no concern to activists. The possibility that the war "caused" the Movement is belied not only by chronology but by the striking absence of any such response to a similar war in the early fifties. And if we read the Port Huron Statement attentively we cannot fail to see that its emphasis falls on problems of collegiate identity and on distaste with the apathetic bourgeois millions. Here was a dissatisfaction *in search of* issues that would allow a stifled idealism to burst forth. The New Left was given its issues, it tried vainly to fashion a stable identity around them, and it spun apart as activists learned one by one that politics could not contain their clamorous feelings.

Although some of the New Left's most fervent apologists have been middle-aged, its psychology has been unmistakably adolescent, with all that this implies about vague yearnings and resentment, loneliness, egoistic thinking, identification with the victimized, and uncertainty of role. Not a radical's age but his degree of participation in this psychology tells us whether he belongs within the Movement. Many student radicals of the sixties, especially among the orthodox Marxists, were relatively exempt from Movement style. The mere fact of having an articulated political vision set the Marxists apart, and their vision was pointedly antipathetic to the visceral politics practiced on the campuses. Where the Movement trusts instinct, Marxists trust theory, acquaintance with the masses, and tactical experience. Marxism's notion of history fosters patience; the Movement is apocalyptic and opposed on principle to postponement of action. The Movement's appropriation of Marx's terms often blurs these distinctions, but radicals who learned their politics from the classic Marxist texts or from scholars such as Mandel, Deutscher, Mills, Williams, Baran and Sweezy, and Magdoff generally lack the Movement's habit of treating personal and public issues as if they were interchangeable.

The New Left as I construe it has always trafficked primarily in symbolism. This fact is clear to anyone who studies Mitchell Goodman's documentary compendium of the Movement, and it is recognized (and instanced) by Peter Marin in the essay that Goodman takes to be the quintessential Movement utterance. "Their specific grievances," says Marin of the young, "are incidental; their real purpose is to make God show his face, to have whatever pervasive and oppressive force makes us perpetual children reveal itself, declare itself, commit itself at last." [3] Those who have worked alongside the Movement for concrete ends, always hoping in vain that activists would learn to keep their hostility focused on the larger issues, will know what Marin means. When the task is to make God show his face the nearest surrogate will do, and it usually turns out to be some hapless college president or dean.

I vividly recall hearing Noam Chomsky plead with Berkeley leftists, in January 1967, to bear in mind the difference between their situation as privileged students and the plight of the decimated Vietnamese. The students listened politely but they were already tired of the "liberal" peace movement and absorbed in fighting imperialism at home by protesting campus rules. A year and a half later Chomsky was shouted down by the striking students at Columbia, who by then were losing all willingness to attach their impulses to commonly accepted goals. In the Weatherman an ultimate disgust with politics emerged. "What was significant for them as revolutionaries," says the Marxist David Horowitz, "was not the political consequence of the deed, but its *karma*. What was important was the *will* to bomb. Revolution here has almost ceased to be a strategy for social change and has become instead a yoga of perfection." [4]

If the Movement makes little sense as politics, it is at least coherent as therapy. What Marin says of himself holds for the New Left at large: "What I am after is an alternative to separation and rage, some kind of connection to things to replace the system of dependence and submission—the loss of self—that now holds sway, slanted toward violence" ("The Open Truth," p. 10). The complaint is not against the oppression and imperialism that form the Movement's manifest concerns, but against bad feelings, "separation and rage" and an anxiety about one's identity. That anxiety is all too plausible in our automated, overorganized age, with its ethic of greed and its humiliation of individuals, not before tyrants and robber barons, but before random stimuli, impersonal procedures, invisible bureaucracies. The Movement shares Ahab's wish to strike through the mask, to locate the absent father and charge him with having caused the unhappiness that now seems to hang in the air without a reason. It is to this end that the *tangibly* oppressed must be courted and mimicked; to feel oneself a part of their cause, to trade one's anxiety for their just anger, is to come into the presence of reality at last. And once one has succeeded in feeling despised rather than simply ignored, one can begin to conceive of a glorious and apocalyptic change of fortune.

Only if we recognize the New Left as a religious venture, "a psychic revolution" as Susan Sontag has called it, can we explain its enthusiasm for thinkers who are, in Sontag's phrase, "not very political"; she lists them as Herbert Marcuse, Norman O. Brown, Norman Mailer, R. D. Laing, Wilhelm Reich, and, on a lesser level of influence, "such openly apolitical, or even reactionary, types as Alan Watts, Leary and McLuhan." [5] These figures share a millenarian style and an absence of definite revolutionary content. The Movement seems scarcely bothered by Reich's veering into McCarthyism or by Brown's explicit anti-Marxism; what counts is the air of drawing up an omnibus indictment of authority. [6] If Marcuse remains the Movement's godfather it is because he has taken the most pains to becloud his misgivings about the juvenile left, yet even thinkers who ignore the Movement altogether can win its sympathy merely by adopting an antinomian and utopian manner. The Movement's taste is for intellectually careless ideologues who diagnose society's neurosis in such drastic terms that no political cure is really imaginable, and word-magic becomes the only recourse. What is required above all is an appearance of proof that the repression of instinct coincides with the repressiveness of capitalist institutions, for then the activist can feel that he is making revolution in the very process of shedding his bourgeois traits.

Radicals sometimes decry this weakness for intellectual sleight-of-hand, yet the Movement as a whole cannot overcome it. To grasp the limitations of the revolutionary quietists is to be thrown back upon traditional structures of knowledge, methodological scruples, and argumentative restraint; but these are exactly what Romantic activists are trying to avoid. "At every step," says Goodman, "we are asked to explain ourselves 'rationally.' That is, we are asked to think in a language—a vocabulary—of rationality that denies feeling—a language eroded and deformed by misuse, and which was formulated by a non-culture that has never undergone our experience" (*The Movement*, p. ix). Rationality is the language of the fathers, the enemies of instinct; in Theodore Roszak's words, "there *must* be an appeal from this reductive rationality which objective consciousness dictates." [7]

Anti-intellectualism, then, is not one of the activists' handicaps but one of their fundamental aims. The Movement strikes Goodman as nothing less than "a force, coming up out of the unconscious, from the gods" (*The Movement*, p. viii), and this force is pitted against an oppressive majority consciousness embracing science, technology, tradition, even logic. According to Roszak the counter culture's project is "to proclaim a new heaven and a new earth so vast, so marvelous that the inordinate claims of technical expertise must of necessity withdraw in the presence of such splendor to a subordinate and marginal status in the lives of men" (*Counter Culture*, p. 240). The mere fact that students find no satisfaction in school suggests to Roszak that the revolution is already at hand, and Susan Sontag too cites "the revolutionary implications of dropping out—of taking drugs (thereby reducing efficiency, clarity, productivity), of disrupting the school system (which furnishes the economy with docile, trained personnel), of concentrating on unproductive hedonistic activities like sex and listening to music" ("Some Thoughts," p. 16). Here is a virtual equation between sabotaging one's intellect and making history. It would be hard to imagine a more patent departure from the coldly rational revolutionism of Marx, Lenin, and Fanon. [8]

It was Marcuse, with his vulgar-Hegelian notion of historical transformation, who most encouraged the Movement to overrate its counter-cultural style. [9] Defining the existing system only in terms of its puritanical ideals, he could consider every instance of deviance as at once a negation of the negation, a return of the repressed, and a concrete argument against his bête noire, scientific positivism. At various points in the sixties Marcuse dallied with the hope that long hair, rock lyrics, homosexuality, even psychosis were signs of capitalism's imminent demise. By combining pedantry, sophistry, and avuncular charm he succeeded in making the rebellious late adolescence of the well-to-do look like a world-historical program instead of a phase. Revolutionism in his hands became a bizarre mixture of ambiguously worded militancy and Romantic hedonism. (The park benches in Hanoi, he gaily observed, are just wide enough to accommodate two lovers.) Reading Marcuse, a young leftist could allow himself to forget the antithesis between the Marxist example of hard work, respect for science and technology, and ideological orthodoxy and the Movement's own blend of libidinal anarchism and "existential" self-absorption.

The New Left's divergence from Marxism is nowhere more apparent than in its thinking about culture. A Marxist such as Lukács or Trotsky regards culture as a product of arduous development, and he sees the revolution's long-run problem as being how to surpass capitalist culture while correcting the injustice that underlies it. One of the classic issues in Marxist social theory is whether the proletariat, having been vaulted to power without any cultural preparation, can achieve a high level of culture before its historical task is finished. No one, however, doubts that the transfer of power and the making of culture are two distinct stages. "We must, first of all," wrote Trotsky, "take possession, politically, of the most important elements of the old culture, to such an extent, at least, as to be able to pave the way for a new culture." [10] The fully human culture predicted by Marx will come into existence when equality, material abundance, and universal education have provided the necessary base.

New Leftists sometimes refer honorifically to such a future, but they are far more interested in undoing their complicity in the existing capitalist culture. The Oedipal politics that enable an activist to feel sorry for himself in the projected form of a ghetto dweller or a Vietnamese peasant also tell him that cul-

ture is a burdensome legacy of the ancestors, a junkpile standing between him and his liberation. Sometimes he expresses
this view directly, attacking the threat to spontaneity posed by
high culture and its spokesmen, who are felt to be snuffing out
youthful rebelliousness by enforcing their doctrines of aesthetic distance, objective contemplation, and a classless, Arnoldian pantheon of masterpieces. More often, the activist
tells himself that culture is preventing someone else's liberation—the ghetto dweller's and the peasant's. "Even when the
humanities and the high culture to which they are devoted are
most radical in content," says one New Leftist, "they are essentially a leisure-class luxury and an enticement away from
the necessity for radical political action." [11] There is so much
penance to be done for "our ineradicable bourgeois upbringing"; we had best "absent ourselves from cultural felicity
awhile" and try to become more like "Huey Newton or Regis
Debray" ("Down with Culture," p. 32). Or perhaps like Sa-
vonarola.

There is, however, a rival notion of culture that catches the
activists' enthusiasm. "We appear to have forgotten in our
schools," says Peter Marin, "what every primitive tribe with
its functional psychology knows: allegiance to the tribe can be
forged only at the deepest levels of the psyche and in extreme
circumstance demanding endurance, daring, and awe; that the
participant must be given *direct* access to the sources of cultural continuity—by and in himself; and that only a place in a
coherent community can be exchanged for a man's allegiance"
("The Open Truth," p. 4). By seeking out "extreme circumstance" and courting danger among a few like-minded friends,
the activist can form a magnetic field of meaning around his
deeds. Instead of abasing himself before objects and ideas he
will be caught up in the energies of his own psyche and feel
himself part of "a live organism" (*The Movement*, p. viii). The
Movement itself will be his culture.

This immersion in the Movement should not be confused

with another project that some radicals find appealing, the rediscovery of folk subcultures that capitalism has bypassed or nearly eradicated. From the New Left standpoint this is just another form of antiquarianism. As Louis Kampf explains,

> the rediscovery of a natural culture cannot provide a cure for the individual's [i.e., the New Leftist's] sense of separation from society. However, given the movement's stress on community, intellectuals may be able to plant their roots in the movement itself. This implies that the movement must become a culture—that is, a way of life. The very forces which have brought about the alienation of intellectuals and the young have propelled us toward that historical moment appropriate for creating a radical culture.[12]

There is thus no need to look anywhere for a culture, provided you belong to the Movement; you yourself will "renovate ways of thinking, feeling, looking and, ultimately, acting" ("Notes," p. 423) in the historical moment that is just arriving, and others can presumably follow along.

As a cultural enterprise, then, the New Left exists not in order to effect political changes, and assuredly not to prepare a base for cultural progress as the Marxists conceive it, but for the sake of its own vitality and emotion. Activists must of course persuade themselves that they are "sharpening contradictions" and "polarizing the masses," but meanwhile they compose what Kampf frankly calls an "elect" with a "secret language" ("Notes," p. 420) that sustains them. Those who know what the Movement is, says Kampf, "are already a part of this culture: they know its private—and rapidly shifting—language; they understand its physical mannerisms; they are wise to its tensions, loves, divisions, and hatreds" ("Notes," p. 420). Feeling oneself to be a member, recognizing one's brothers and sisters by their most up-to-date affectations, appears to have largely replaced political success as a focus of satisfaction.

"The radical Movement of the '60's," as Andrew Kopkind

has perceived, "developed a kind of Ptolemaic theory of the political universe: everything is in orbit around *my* movement, around *my* politics, around *my* collective" ("The Greening," p. 52). The Movement renders cultural issues invisible by admitting them only as future tasks for its members to work out within their lives. In place of dead objects we will have live actions, and those actions can symbolically expiate "the crimes, the human suffering" ("Notes," p. 424) that have buttressed the specious official culture. "Not a performance should go by without disruption," says Kampf of Lincoln Center. "The fountains should be dried with calcium chloride, the statuary pissed on, the walls smeared with shit" ("Notes," p. 426). Lincoln Center will still be surrounded by a ghetto but Movement activists will be doing their thing, and *that* is genuine culture.

If New Left fraternalism is an end in itself, we can appreciate why activists find much to engage them in their home base, the university. Just about every aspect of the academic environment impresses them as an attempt to rob them of brotherhood, and chief among such devices are the repressive ideals of disinterestedness and rational debate. The ideals themselves—not merely the Cold War perversion of them—are felt to threaten the Movement by proposing a rival basis of association and belief. An instrumental organization like ROTC can be met on its own ground, for the Movement shares its conception of the university's purpose; but what can be done about "self-selected authorities" (*Counter Culture*, p. 263) who claim that scientific logic stands above all organizations? The community of scholars, even radical scholars, reeks of paternal authoritarianism and must be replaced by a community of activists who already know the necessary truths about genocide and resistance, liberal fascism and freedom, the pigs and the people.[13]

There are obvious limits to the candor an activist can exercise in writing, or even thinking, about the egoistic basis of his culture. To realize that he has joined a vanguard without any possibility of a following would abruptly end his revolutionary dream. Simply to be a pisser of statues is not enough. The most admired Movement documents are therefore those that exhort activists to take their message to the people, who have been numbed and harangued by the ruling class's media and do not yet understand that student leftists are their friends. Even the despised bourgeoisie, say these documents, is suffering amid its surfeit of gadgets and will benefit from learning about consumerism, surplus repression, and repressive desublimation. The better Movement essays have a Grecian-urn quality: the activists and the masses are always just about to embrace.

Hence the appeal of the most famous New Left cultural manifesto, John McDermott's "The Laying On of Culture." [14] Universities, says McDermott, are prime reinforcers of the "hierarchic tendencies implicit in the social and economic system" (p. 299), and one of their chief instruments is the idea of culture—specifically, the belief that culture "includes the Western Heritage, the Western Tradition, the Literary Tradition, the traditions of reason and civility, etc., and that these are most fully embodied in the profession of academe and the written treasures of which academe is priestly custodian and inspired interpreter" (p. 300). Before this sentence is halfway finished we have realized that "culture" is an unspeakable affront to the people. But McDermott is politic. He is not, he says, attacking Western culture and scholarship, but only their implications for working-class students who are being systematically humiliated by their teachers in community colleges. These students are essentially colonials, destined to fill deadening jobs near the base of the technocracy, and their introduction to cultural masterpieces is really intended to strip them of local and class pride. To avoid this fate they will require "critical universities, liberation courses, seminars in local and working-class history" (p. 301), and similar measures

which, as McDermott implies, can be stimulated by the Movement teachers who are fanning across the country from their
graduate schools.

The beauty of this argument is its semblance of egali-
tarianism. McDermott has found a real phenomenon that bears
scrutiny, the use of community colleges as implements of social channeling, and he seems eager to help a neglected group
of citizens become whatever they please. Oddly, however, his
harshest comments are directed not against policies but
against diffuse "hierarchic tendencies" that are chiefly instanced in the teaching of literature. Like all New Left anti-
authoritarianism, McDermott's is at once global and parochial,
challenging all oppression everywhere (in the capitalist world)
while coming down hardest on the relatively insignificant
abuses that are closest to home. What he has brought to the
academic hinterlands is simply his concern to put down the
English professors back at the university.

I doubt whether much animus against hierarchy as such is
harbored by the upwardly mobile working people who have
made their way into the community colleges; this passion is
restricted to disaffected intellectuals in search of proletarian
moorings. A leftist who pondered such a difference of outlook
and admitted the class basis of his own unfocused rage would
immediately graduate from the Movement, but McDermott's
course is rather to consider how the children of workers can be
brought around to his sophomoric ideas about liberation.
These students are, for the duration of his essay, not real people but agents of a shadowy campaign against power. The abstract severity of the analysis forecloses any possibility that
some of them might *want* to expose themselves to nonlocal culture or to occupy a different social class. They are domestic
"natives" one and all, and if they are reluctant to resent this
status it must be because they have not yet found their Che
Guevaras, namely McDermott and the other radicals he is addressing. McDermott encourages the knowledgeable activist to

become a missionary, bringing Samuel Gompers and John L. Lewis to the unwashed while casting out the heathen idol Shakespeare. Who, then, is laying what on whom?

When the New Left trains its attention directly on literature and literary study, the result is a combination of Lawrentian and moralistic demands. What we require from art, according to Theodore Roszak, is "the white-hot experience of authentic vision that might transform our lives and, in so doing, set us at warlike odds with the dominant culture" (*Counter Culture*, p. 257).[15] The implication is that without such a boost from the arts we will be left immobile. The point, as always with the New Left, is to sustain the Movement's own spirit—"a spirit," Mitchell Goodman explains, "that inter-plays in many bodies, that come together as they move and touch, and give one another warmth, hope" (*The Movement*, p. vii). Hence the importance of keeping clear of the literary professors, whose specialty is draining away the vital juices from everything they touch, and hence too the necessity of avoiding those works that are sedative to begin with. The more politically minded wing of the Movement puts the matter in ideological terms borrowed from conventional revolutionism: we need books that were written from a liberated perspective, books that side unambiguously with the oppressed.

Unfortunately, not many works can be found to pass this test. Some of the promising candidates are tainted by their membership in that abomination, the Western Heritage, and they generally smack of "ruler morality."[16] "Whom did the values represented by Homer's Achilles serve?" asks Louis Kampf. "Are we to take the reactionary and mercenary objectives of Balzac [Marx's favorite novelist: F. C.] as merely an adjunct to his artistry? We take the concept of tragedy to represent the West's most profound understanding of man's place in the world. Yet is its counter-revolutionary acceptance of fate something we are supposed to teach as a received value?"[17]

It would be pointless to reply that these questions confound literature with propaganda and teaching with indoctrination, for Kampf wants to be disburdened of all such nice distinctions. The ego functions that might enable him to grasp that a work of art is only a hypothetical world, and a potential occasion for exercising the mind rather than brutalizing it, have been exposed and denounced as part of the capitalist apparatus of thought control. Literature is now regarded as a set of land mines, nearly all of which have been laid in the Movement's path by the ruling class, which is considered to have preserved its reactionary continuity from Homer's day to the present. In his search for acceptable texts Kampf is finally reduced to proposing Chairman Mao's poems about the Long March and even his "political formulas," which "may be simple, naïve, unsubtle, devoid of tragic doubt—but they happen to be true" ("The Trouble," p. 32).

There are, naturally, various possible attitudes for a radical to take toward literature. Marxists have their own, rather jesuitical, excuse for reading the classics as part of their prehistory. Some radicals take an interest in the efforts of Artaud, Brecht, and the Surrealists to help smash the bourgeoisie by alarming its sensibility. Others, including Marcuse, justify eclecticism by pleading that the classics are more rebellious than you might suppose.[18] And some leftists, concurring with Marx himself in this regard, actually think that literature is one thing and revolution another. But none of these attitudes, least of all Marx's, captures the New Left program of *replacing* literary culture with activism. Louis Kampf (currently President of the Modern Language Association) thus spoke for much of the Movement when he proclaimed that "the *study* of literature—the voyeurism implicit in this—must really come to an end if all of us are to be full participants in the making of our culture" ("The Trouble," p. 34).

The New Left view of literary criticism, though it follows logically from Kampf's position, may seem incomprehensible unless we bear in mind the Movement's belief that everything is either part of the solution or part of the problem. That is, propositions about literature are really attempts to subvert or enhance social change. The modern shibboleths of irony, complexity, and ambiguity are thus exposed as devices for downgrading revolutionary authors and for inculcating resignation. The matter is settled as soon as the conservative and agrarian leanings of some of the founders of New Criticism have been cited, for a critic's class affiliation is considered the most reliable clue to the meaning of his remarks about poetry. New Criticism, says Bruce Franklin, triumphed along with McCarthyism and represented an attempt to "sweep the field of literary study of any relevance to contemporary life." [19] Viewed in the light of Vietnam—and the New Left views everything in this light—the New-Critical attempt to reconcile tensions amounts to "murder" (DiSalvo, "This Murder," p. 11). And the same judgment applies to all other schools of commentary that dwell on form and value instead of on the relevant social issues.[20] Criticism is worse than superfluous anyway, for we already know that real (collective) creativity aims not at producing beautiful artifacts but at liberating people from the bourgeois mentality; and the latter is typified precisely in the fussiness of "critical insights."

The aesthetic and political implications of this attitude come across vividly in an essay on Cuban literature by Roberta Salper, who was recently elected to the Executive Council of the MLA.[21] Her argument is framed with sayings of Marcuse's from *An Essay on Liberation* and "Repressive Tolerance," and she adopts Marcuse's view that freedom of imagination in our time is threatened, not by anything so crude as censorship, but by rationality in the service of profit, by consumerism, by the near-impossibility of mounting an effective political protest, and by tolerance itself. Tolerance, she has learned from Marcuse, is the principle under which "a magazine prints both a negative and positive report on the FBI" (p. 29) and thereby disguises its oneness with that very organization. "In aesthetic terms," she explains, "this ethic of objectivity or 'benevolent neutrality' has meant an ability to absorb and neutralize even the most radical of formal experiments. Socialist Realism is an overreaction to this liberal tolerance and credo of 'impartiality' " (p. 29).

Socialist Realism, which became the Union of Soviet Writers' fearsome theme in 1932, happened in fact to be a bureaucratic "overreaction" to the last vestiges of artistic freedom in Russia. It is strange to find this doctrine, under which thousands of writers and artists were exiled and murdered, interpreted as a wholesome though possibly imprudent reply to Western eclecticism.[22] What the author means, however, is that she herself is prepared to overreact to the maddening blandness of American policy toward dissent. True aesthetic freedom as expounded by Marcuse, she says, is simply the freedom to imagine a society entirely different from our own— but how can we realize such freedom when our government refuses to manifest its essential bias? ". . . A free society in Marcuse's terms," explains Salper, "demands a sensitivity free from the repressive satisfactions of the unfree societies . . ." (p. 17). Still following Marcuse, she concludes that left-propagandistic art is really the freest sort because it helps us to picture a better social order.

With her definitions thus squared away, Salper can give an unclouded survey of the Cuban literary scene. She finds it heartening that Cuban writers are sometimes forced to work in the factories and fields "so they will learn what needs to be communicated and to whom" (p. 30n.); she marvels at Fidel's magnanimity in proposing not to suppress any books that are loyal to the revolution (no others can be published); she sympathetically explains the Culture Council's objections to Heberto Padilla's scandalous "concern with 'individualism' and 'liberty' in a pre-revolutionary sense" (p. 24); and she hails Cuban censorship for its hearty openness, so unlike the "more or less hidden censorship" (p. 30) which, in our own country, takes the insidious form of protecting dissident statements without offering them prime media time. "Censorship in Cuba still serves to protect and preserve society," she concedes, "but it is not a repressive society, vitiating life instincts and isolating human beings from one another, from their political existence" (p. 30). Unlike Castro himself, who until recently was apologetic about the need for any antilibertarian measures, the author is thus disposed to favor them on principle as constituting part of a thoroughgoing antithesis to her surroundings. No one actually living under a dictatorship could imagine that official control over the arts is a boon to the life instincts. This soap bubble can only be lofted in a climate of bourgeois individualism, when radicals have begun to confound freedom with the overcoming of loneliness.

A casual reader of Salper's essay might miss her Romantic emphasis on the buried self and conclude that she is an outright Stalinist; careless or disingenuous analysts have made just that misjudgment of the New Left as a whole. The point of worshiping Cuba's fraternal politicization of literature is simply to arm one's mind against the suffocating pluralism under which one continues to live at home. The literary leftist's conduct in his university sufficiently reveals that, far from being a Stalinist, he is obsessed with the contaminating effect of all power, including his own as a teacher.

There are, to be sure, scattered bits of contrary evidence. Our students, says Louis Kampf, "*will have to* oppose the system of acculturation and spiritual servitude which our colleges encourage." [23] As for his colleagues, Kampf in an early essay envisioned a lockstep faculty of leftists who would implement the Movement line: "Departments of literature will have to look on themselves as . . . part of a front dedicated to the human ends of poetry. . . . Their critical function will be to expose the enemies of literature with the light of reason and to destroy them with the passion of moral concern." [24] This, however, was only a passing Zhdanovite dream, out of keeping not only with the New Left's political weakness but also with its anarchism. The Movement professor more typically uses his limited academic authority to undermine the university's legitimacy in minor ways (giving all students the same grade, cancelling classes to honor leftist festivals, substituting Movement topics for the announced subject matter, joining sit-ins against the president, etc.), always in the expectation that "repression" will ensue and that everyone standing between him and his persecutors will have to choose sides. The activist embarks on these struggles half knowing that he is going to lose. Whatever else this is, it isn't Stalinism.

Only while standing at the students' side, it would seem, can the activist professor feel untroubled by his own authority. The teacher-student relationship in its ordinary form floods him with guilt. Kampf reports that he, like his students, can only tolerate his own teaching when a creative disruption occurs—as, for example, when a two-hour debate about why one student was sitting on the floor without any clothes on provided "the only lively discussion we had all semester," or when, in a dreary seminar on Proust, the students "decided" participatorily to reconvene at the M.I.T. Student Center, which had been unilaterally "declared" a sanctuary for a military deserter, and suddenly "Proust's sensibility became politicized for us" ("The Trouble," pp. 33, 34). (It is a shame that Proust, with his supreme taste for incongruities, could not have lived to see his languors so improved.) In both cases tedium was conquered by a nullifying of the teacher-student hierarchy and the formation of a community of people who were all, for a brief period, upset about the same thing. Literature is useful to such a community only insofar as it bolsters morale, and perhaps the worst thing for that morale would be overscrupulous regard for what an author actually wrote.

There remains the problem of what to do with literature between demonstrations. The New Left can't dwell on the superiority of one work to another, for, says Kampf, all such judgments derive from competition and commerce. The very circulation of literature, to say nothing of its publication, strikes him as a step toward commodity fetishism ("The Trouble," p. 34). Even the seemingly innocent fact that novels have usually been "written by one individual working in isolation for the consumption of another individual, likewise reading in the isolation of his or her room" ("The Trouble," p. 30), violates the necessary group spirit. The depressing thing about verbal art is that it wallows unashamedly in fantasy, turning the imagination inward "rather than outward, toward worldly activity" ("The Trouble," p. 34). The more he thinks about it, the more the activist professor feels like a preacher who finds himself married to a whore—and obliged to drum up business for her among the congregation. No wonder Kampf is prompted to suspect that resistance to the dominant culture is "madness." Yet "the only real choice may be whether to be mad (though civilized) on society's terms, or on one's own" ("The Humanities," p. 312).

Professors who have found themselves briefly outflanked by New Leftists in their departments or in the MLA have feared a takeover of the discipline, and in the ensuing hysteria even mild criticism of "English" for its political provincialism has been greeted as advocating a Bolshevik reign. What is truly worrisome is not this implausible specter but the fact that academic people continue to be dumbstruck by absurd arguments. The New Left, along with the rest of the burgeoning counter culture, has shown itself incapable of tolerating the moral indeterminacy of art and the intellectual dizziness of knowing that one doesn't know. Perhaps a decade back, when a good number of people still assumed that the criticism and teaching of literature were worthwhile activities, the irrationalist faction would simply have had to take one path and the English departments another. No one is quite so sure now; "English" has lost its nerve.

The reasons for this development are only partly known,

and they probably extend to such varied and uncontrollable phenomena as the ascendancy of visual media, the enervated frivolity of much contemporary literature, the rise of the "service station" multiversity, the loss of human scale as a result of technology, and the disorientation of aesthetic and moral impulses in an age of routine terror and cosmic banality, of televised war from Asia and televised golf from the moon. Then, too, there is the counter culture itself, which has taught even some of the professors to hang loose and let it be—or at least to annotate the Beatles instead of their former texts. Their success in keeping pace with fashion has drawn them farther from their old sense of working on problems whose interest lay in their very subtlety and exactingness. To some extent the profession already shares the New Left's embarrassment in the presence of merely aesthetic issues.

No one, then, is to blame for the apparent decline of literary study. The right question to ask is whether we ought to care. The standard academic reply to utilitarian detractors, that objective knowledge is a sufficient end in itself, doesn't carry much conviction in this instance. No one really thinks that new outpourings of fact and opinion about the dog-eared classics will be valuable simply because they are knowledge, and there is nothing precious about a person's ability to be unprejudiced about works that have long since ceased to interest him. Nor, of course, are most professors so politically neutral as they think. Lacking awareness of their politics as readers, they cannot refute the New Left's wild assertion that literary study is all politics anyway—first yours and now ours.

There is probably no way to make a convincing defense of any of the humanities except by showing, through committed practice, that the discipline is still meaningful to oneself. The question of whether the results of this practice are needed can only be parried: what we emphatically don't need is a society in which somebody's politicized idea of need determines whether a given activity is allowed to continue. Having made that minimal stand, we could add that the humanities are precisely those disciplines that search for value. The effective disappearance of literary study would imply that the society no longer sought value from literature; people would have decided that all the relevant norms were fully known or not worth knowing in view of our helplessness before events. Such a society could no longer be called free.

Literary study, then, may not yield especially useful findings, but at its best it fosters an important kind of engagement, a disposition to risk being changed by lending oneself to a problematic experience. This quality is what Sartre means by "generosity":

> Reading is an exercise in generosity, and what the writer requires of the reader is not the application of an abstract freedom but the gift of his whole person, with his passions, his prepossessions, his sympathies, his sexual temperament, and his scale of values. . . . But he does not stop there; he also requires that [readers] recognize his creative freedom, and that they in turn solicit it by a symmetrical and inverse appeal.[25]

Where such generosity is lacking we find either pedantry or its left-wing counterpart, relevance. That is, we find one way or another of ensuring that nothing will be learned but inessential reinforcements of what one already knows, or thinks he knows.

If English studies remain more than superficially alive, it is because people still feel a challenge to test their evolving sensibilities, including their sense of politics, against works that can answer—not simply confirm—whatever expectations are brought to them. Literary study at its best sharpens our awareness of the boundaries between literature and our predispositions, enabling us to have a colloquy with sources of meaning that will never be fully assimilated. Both the pedant and the activist abolish one of the parties to this colloquy. The irony in the activist's case is that his hope in removing boundaries is to feel less severed from meaning, less alone. What he finds instead is that his remedy for separation and rage is worse than the disease: he has turned the world into an echo chamber resounding with slogans. Then his complaints about oppression, though still misplaced, are finally commensurate with the gravity of his plight, for a man who can no longer respond to the freedom of others has lost his own freedom as well.

Chapter Eight

ANXIOUS ENERGETICS

In the early 1970's the overt, activist radicalism that I had responded to so ambivalently appeared to be transmuting itself into quasi-scientific and "spiritual" forms. In California especially, revolutionism was going therapeutic, and the once-neglected figure of Wilhelm Reich was beginning to look paradigmatic in several respects. With his personal break from Freud and then his passage from Marxist agitation to a materialistic body mysticism, Reich epitomized the yearnings and intellectual shortcuts I most wanted to assess. Here as in the preceding essay, consideration of an extremist movement prompted me to underscore longstanding but hitherto tacit commitments to reason and democratic process.

*"Words can be relied upon only
so long as one is sure that their
function is to reveal and not to conceal."*
Hannah Arendt

*U*ntil fairly recently it seemed apparent that Wilhelm
Reich, though a persistent presence in "left" or "advanced"
circles since the 1940's, was fated eventually to be dismissed as
a minor curiosity of American cultural history. The founder of
character analysis and orgonomy, who died in 1957 after being
imprisoned as a cancer quack, has never been entirely forgotten, either as a therapeutic innovator or as a prophet of sexual
freedom. But the most prominent and sophisticated Reichians
of the postwar period either gradually lost interest in his ideas
or felt required to hedge them with major reservations, and
Reich became a remote and implausible figure whose zealous
advocacy of the orgasm seemed more quaint that courageous.

Now, however, in a distinctly altered cultural atmosphere,
Reich has begun to find something like the broad following he
always expected. Political radicals and ex-radicals, whose
hopes for a better society have become increasingly focused on
an end to neurosis, admire him not only for his stand against
capitalism and patriarchy, but for his rejection of "adjustment" as a therapeutic goal. Orgonomy and its offshoot "activity therapies" are attracting favorable notice from psychia-
trists and psychologists who feel that psychoanalysis has
proved itself too cumbersome and cautious for purposes of
broad social hygiene. Reich's scientific propositions, once generally ridiculed, are the subject of numerous conferences and
seminars. His major writings have been reissued in hardcover
and paper editions, and he is himself the topic of other books,
one of which implicitly ranks him in influence, if not in merit,
among the "Modern Masters." Reich's particular version of
antinomianism seems well suited to what one conference bro-

chure calls "today's emphasis on sexual, political, and spiritual liberation." [1]

To some extent it might be said that Reich's own ideas helped to bring about the climate in which he is now being rehabilitated. Some of the radical intellectuals who had been drawn to his work in the forties became themselves propagators of body-centered therapy, uncoercive education, antiauthoritarian politics, and an ideology of dionysiac individualism. In England, A. S. Neill welcomed Reich as a philosophical ally in his efforts to promote the self-regulation and free development of children. In America, Paul Goodman and Frederick Perls used Reich, not Freud, as their point of departure when they fashioned Gestalt therapy; and Goodman, Dwight MacDonald, and others, accepting the Reichian insight that "a coercive society depends upon instinctual repression," [2] invoked Reich as the patron of a sensuous and decentralized new politics. In addition, Reich was admired for diverse reasons by Saul Bellow, Isaac Rosenfeld, Norman Mailer, Allen Ginsberg, Jack Kerouac, and William Burroughs. Although none of these writers forwarded the more practical aspects of orgonomy, all of them can be presumed to have influenced the development of a "Reichian" cultural atmosphere.

If the early phase of Reichianism can teach us anything about the present one, it is that ideological and temperamental affinities are likely to be more important that intellectual agreement with Reich's ideas. In the forties and fifties those ideas were largely untested and only vaguely understood by many of Reich's most ardent followers. Psychological and political radicals turned to Reich not because they found him a more careful student of the world than Marx and Freud, but because they felt historically disinherited and stymied. By the forties Freudian doctrine, which had once seemed so exhilaratingly resistant to every form of authority, was suspected of conformist tendencies, and so in a grimmer sense was Marxism in its Stalinist guise. In the gloom of the Cold War years, intellectuals whose historicism had been shaken faced the choice of either accommodating themselves to a prosperous anti-Communist society or taking a stand directly on what Mailer, citing Reich, called "the rebellious imperatives of the self." [3] It was evidently Reich's irrefutably vague optimism, rather than his specific notions about orgasm or work democracy or orgone energy, that answered the embattled radicals' mood. As Theodore Solotaroff has said of Isaac Rosenfeld, "The very extremism of Reich's system—as over against the Freudian—must have commended it in this time of extremity . . ." [4] To be a Reichian, with or without acceptance of Reich's claim to have discovered the life force in Cosmic Orgone Energy, was to seek contact with Mailer's "God . . . located in the senses of [one's] body, that trapped, mutilated and nonetheless megalomaniacal God who is It, who is energy, life, sex, force, the Yoga's *prana,* the Reichian's orgone, Lawrence's 'blood,' Hemingway's 'good' . . ." (*Advertisements,* p. 325). In Mailer's hands the orgasmic principle became a license to hurl oneself against "every social restraint and category," to break "those mutually contradictory inhibitions against violence and love which civilization has exacted of us" (*Advertisements,* pp. 328, 318).

This same diffuse rebelliousness still animates many Reichians, especially those political activists of the sixties who, like their thwarted counterparts after World War II, have been regrouping around the banner of "radical psychiatry." They too, it seems, respond more to Reich's mood of visionary defiance than to the fine points of orgonomy. So do radical feminists like Kate Millett and Juliet Mitchell, who value Reich (with stern qualifications) for prefiguring their own stance against patriarchal oppression. [5]

Yet we can no longer be so certain that Reich's current appeal is entirely ideological. In contrast to the early admirers who had only an approximate sense of his scientific claims, many now argue in detail that he was primarily a great investigator of nature. Instead of observing the once-customary practice of distinguishing between "constructive" and "wild" phases in Reich's career, they tend to embrace it in its entirety, excepting only the last four or five years in which Reich, by then unquestionably paranoid, fancied himself a messenger from outer space and a veteran of interplanetary war. Even the most moderate of Reich's recent exegetes, such as W. Edward Mann and David Boadella, are ready to defend not only the relatively accessible ideas about character armor and the orgasm reflex, but the whole chain of Reich's subsequent assertions about electrophysiology, plasma flow, radiation, cancer pathology, weather control, and so forth.[6]

By far the best case for this new assessment is the one made by Boadella, who, by tracing Reich's career from each hypothesis to the next and recapitulating the conditions and results of his major experiments—meanwhile documenting the often shameful tactics of his opponents—shows the logical and evidential basis of ideas that might otherwise look like sheer science fiction. Reich, Boadella maintains, was drawn reluctantly to his conclusions by unanticipated, unanswerable findings. Those conclusions, he says, may have been only approximate first efforts, but the findings remain and must be dealt with by anyone who would challenge Reich's credibility. Where the original reports and case studies are missing, blame must be laid on the American government for the indiscriminate book-burning that was inflicted on Reich in 1956. And as for the prima facie implausibility of one man's making major breakthroughs in psychiatry, physiology, chemistry, biology, medicine, meteorology, physics, and astronomy, we must suspend judgment and grant Reich the synthetic nature of his enterprise. As an "energetic functionalist" Reich looked for unifying principles that would characterize life in all its forms. There is every reason to suppose that such principles exist, and no reason to doubt that they could be at least roughly sketched by a genius who devoted thirty years to isolating them. The clinching argument, for Mann as well as Boadella, is that later, independent researches in ionization, cosmic rays, geomagnetic forces, pollution, body auras, and psychosomatic medicine have turned up hard facts that Reich had been getting at in his idiosyncratic way.

My own ignorance of laboratory procedures, combined with my sense that normal science is moving rapidly toward integrative understanding of life processes and even toward rapprochement with elements of "the occult," makes me hesitate to criticize this reasoning. Reich has at least been vindicated in overriding the conventional borders between mind and body and in depicting all creatures as energy fields interacting with energy streams of cosmic origin. Some Reichian ideas that were dismissed as primitivism by Philip Rieff and Charles Rycroft now seem much less outlandish than they did just a few years ago. Nor do I wish to deny that many of the effects Reich observed may have been real. On the contrary, the one incontestable fact about Reich is that he was a charismatic person in whose presence odd things tended to happen, not just to himself but to experimental subjects and witnesses. (Whether he made sufficient allowance for this exceptional influence in drawing laws from his experience is another question.) It seems fair to think of Reich as a figure comparable to Franz Mesmer, who, in another century dominated by mechanistic physics, correctly emphasized the importance of energy transactions which neither he nor anyone else could reconcile with existing knowledge.

To see Reich in these terms, however, is not at all to settle the issue of his cultural or ideological meaning. Like Mesmer himself, Reich owes his popularity not to the approval of scientific colleagues, but to the charm his ideas exert on people who are generally sympathetic to life-affirming and unitary theories—in a word, to romantics. Efforts like Boadella's to assimilate Reich's work to the perspective of normal science may obscure the fact that Reichianism has been in several ways an *anti*-scientific movement, holding out promises that are seductive precisely because of the contrast they make with the austerity and fragmented awareness of science as usually practiced. As a structure of postulates orgonomy is open to the charge of tautology, but this apparent defect can be an advantage to people who want their revolutionary certitude kept secure from intrusion.

Reich was remarkably candid about the unorthodox relation between his findings and his presuppositions. He observed that his experiments were directed, not merely toward testing his hypotheses, but above all toward suppressing his misgivings about them. He mustered the courage "to go on in spite of disturbing and apparently negative findings in control experiments; not to invalidate new facts with superficial controls; *always to check negative control findings personally*; and, finally, not to give in to the temptation of saying, 'It was just an illusion' " (*SW*, p. 206; italics in original). When traditional methods and devices failed to detect the phenomena Reich believed in, he resorted to "special, hitherto unknown, methods and research procedures" that would yield the desired results (*SW*, p. 196). Believing that *"man cannot feel or imagine anything that has no real, objective existence in one form or another"* (*SW*, p. 210; italics in original), he found his proofs in such subjective impressions as his subordinates' headaches, the appearance of spots before his closed eyes, otherwise unaccountable feelings of rage, and an absence of "sparkle" in the landscape. Even allowing for the handicaps of exile and persecution under which Reich operated, we have to notice a strong element of wishfulness in these practices.

Then, too, there was Reich's eccentric way of shielding his supposed discoveries from criticism. As Ola Raknes naïvely states,

> One of the common criticisms against Reich was that, instead of repeating and varying an experiment so as to detect any possible source of error, "as scientists should do," he would trust his

findings, as soon as he had been able to place them in some rational connection, and go on to new discoveries. What his critics did not know was that in most cases he would keep his discoveries to himself, sometimes for years, until they led him to new discoveries, which was his criterion for the validity of a finding.[7]

Reich, in other words, hid his experimental results from the scientific community while using them as a basis for further inferences, then taking the latter as confirmation of the former. This combination of secretiveness and dogmatism constituted a fundamental break with the empirical spirit—a spirit, we should note, whose cardinal point isn't the forming of hypotheses based on observation, but the submitting of those hypotheses to the fullest scrutiny according to agreed-upon criteria of adequacy.[8]

The keystone of Reich's science is an unwillingness to be judged by rational skepticism. That skepticism, because it remains unmoved by "subjective organ sensations" (*SW*, p. 209), is itself condemned as a debility of overcivilization. "It is those who feel only very little or nothing at all," says Boadella, "who need most desperately to deny the existence of an energy which, once accepted, would make obvious the fact that their organ sensations were seriously disturbed." [9] Hence no one outside Reich's purified circle of believers can be trusted as a critic of orgonomy. When such intruders do presume to attack Reich, they are merely displaying their own orgastic deficiency.[10] Only those whose "own organismic energy can function freely" (Raknes, p. 50) deserve to be heard, and this free functioning—reachable by inhibited moderns through the one avenue of orgone treatment—produces a new style of sensuous knowing. Instead of abstractly investigating the world, the adept lives with the truth as a practical mystic,[11] listening to the "objectively expressive language" of orgonotic streamings (*RSF*, p. 63n.).

This is not to say, however, that orgonomy makes its claims on a forthrightly mystical basis. Reich always insisted that he was a strict materialist who had, to his own satisfaction at least, demonstrated his propositions. No one ever maintained more adamantly that all phenomena are physical and that all philosophy is illusion; the Blakean rules Reich detected in the universe were presented as mere inferences from meter readings. This double emphasis, at once hortatory and positivistic, gave Reich a rhetorical advantage over avowedly antiscientific thinkers. Orgonomy amounts to what Michael Polanyi, thinking of Marxism, defined as a dynamo-objective coupling, in which "Alleged scientific assertions, which are accepted as such because they satisfy moral passions, will excite these passions further, and thus lend increased convincing power to the scientific affirmations in question—and so on, indefinitely." As Polanyi adds, "such a dynamo-objective coupling is also potent in its own defence. Any criticism of its scientific part is rebutted by the moral passion behind it, while any moral objections to it are coldly brushed aside by invoking the inexorable verdict of its scientific findings." [12]

The analogy with Marxism is not a casual one. Reich was among other things a theorist of dialectical materialism who, for a while at least, reflected all the sanguine historicism of the original Marxist vision. Like his old Berlin comrade Arthur Koestler, he didn't simply evolve into a fervent anti-Communist when history failed to obey the script, but also sublimated his transcendent expectations into "revolutionary" scientific doctrine. The exit from history that Marx had posited in temporal terms as the proletariat's eventual triumph was transposed into a repeal of the laws of physical necessity, and the now-dubious power of the masses became the power—sexual, perceptual, even mystical—of the sufficient self. Unlike Koestler, however, Reich continued to present himself as an explicitly political revolutionary, thus sparing his followers the necessity of choosing between Tamburlaine and Faust. Somehow the spread of erotic freedom and the harnessing of orgone energy would result in an end to capitalism and patriarchy—the very outcome that seemed unreachable through traditional means of struggle. Meanwhile the secondary benefits of revolutionism, such as elite membership, privileged insight, a sense of evangelical mission, and faith in the future, could be found in a movement organized around supposed truths about nature.

The rallying point of Reich's new creed was the orgasm, an eloquent choice on several counts. In the first place, the experience is a private one, in marked contrast to the proletariat's assumption of state power. In a time of shattered public expectations, local orgastic success or the illusion of it can be taken as proof that the revolution is going forward after all. Again, as an immediate and total release of tension, the orgasm is an ideal vehicle for a drastically compressed historicism: the fulfillment that was to have worked itself out through decades of class struggle becomes a matter of personal ecstasy. The orgasm, furthermore, is defined in part as a blotting-out of consciousness—inevitably including consciousness of setbacks in more orthodox political ventures. We have already seen how Reich's subjectivist posture insulates his whole system from criticism. Within that system the mute and obliterative orgasm serves as a refuge from unwelcome surprises, pessimistic reflections, fruitless calculation—even from language itself, the medium of thinking too precisely on the event.

The flight from language and intellection becomes especially pertinent when we consider the centrality of Reich's quarrel with Freud. Orgonomy was devised as an inversion not of Marxism but of psychoanalysis, the talking cure, in which "making the unconscious conscious" is the therapeutic aim. That aim obviously depends on a broader consensus that rationality and control are worth striving for. By putting the orgasm in the place of self-knowledge, Reich addresses not only thwarted radicals and scarred veterans of psychoanalysis, but many others who now feel that rational consciousness and inhibition are synonymous. The fortunes of orgonomy see. tied to the currency of this sentiment more than any other.

Thus Reich has become the posthumous beneficiary of a widespread demoralization in our culture, a weakening of the once-axiomatic belief that conduct should be guided by reason. In a subtle and paradoxical way, that belief had already been eroded by Freud, who honored it with such apparent tenacity. It was Reich's destiny to expose the ethical ambiguity of Freud's psychology and to resolve it on the side of irrationalism. For people who want to forsake neither their insurrectionary sentiments nor their yearning for transcendent meaning, Reich held out desublimation as a quasi-religious goal.

Modern psychologies in general, as the successors to a moribund faith, have tried not simply to describe how mental equilibrium is maintained, but to put forward that equilibrium as an ethical ideal, persuading a restless, doctrinally confused public that sanity in this world, though more problematical than anyone once supposed, is in itself a worthy goal of striving.[13] The full difficulty of this project can be observed in the stoic Freud, who urged us to restrain our impulses but denied that we possess a native conscience; who made self-knowledge his ideal but characterized the mind as a self-deceiving organ; and who plunged us into the chthonian unconscious while steadfastly maintaining the humdrum secular norm of healthy functioning. In his role as ironic physician Freud refused to set his sights beyond what he called ordinary human unhappiness, but as a Nietzschean *conquistador*, challenging the whole basis of Western conscious rationality, he encouraged utopian speculations about abolishing repression. In retrospect it seems inevitable that ideologies such as Reich's would rush in to satisfy the appetite for catharsis that Freud had both whetted and disdained.

When Reich described himself as the one faithful interpreter of libido theory he was making a perfectly cogent claim. What

he did was to pick up the mechanistic side of Freud's thought
and accept its consequences unreservedly. It was Freud, not
Reich, who first supposed that all mental acts were theoretically traceable to missed gratification, and who posited the
idea of "actual neuroses" stemming from dammed-up libido.
It was also Freud who extended psychoanalytic speculation to
prehistory and the cellular level; whose notion of the superego
implied that social compliance comes about through the in-
ternalization of paternal castration threats; and whose account
of culture depicted every gain for order as stolen from sexuality. Reich's instinctual demonology is recognizably Freud's
own, set loose from the misgivings that prompted Freud to su-
perimpose a vocabulary of motives on his vocabulary of ca-
thexes. It merely remained for Reich to ideologize tension
release as a *summum bonum* which, in the light of Freud's own
energy hydraulics, could be attained through removal of every
social demand upon the individual.

Thus Reich's disagreement with Freud can be understood as
an endorsement of extremist implications in Freud's own
thought. Freud's retraction, in the 1920's, of the idea that all
anxiety was blocked libido signified a retreat from an exclusively sexual etiology of the neuroses—a retreat that Reich interpreted in political terms as an accommodation to a repressive society. Whether or not he was correct in this inference,
Reich himself assuredly had extrascientific reasons for insist-
ing that the original "quantitative factor" be retained. Libido,
after all, was a metaphorical concept, not a physical substance
that could be observed by either Freud or Reich. When Freud
downplayed libido he was making room for an ego psychology
of motives, defenses, and adaptations; when Reich championed libido he was rejecting all such mentalistic categories
so as to retain a determinism with eschatological implications.
If neuroses were caused by sexual deprivation alone, then one
could lay all blame for unhappiness on the (paternal) inhibi-
tors of sexuality, speak confidently about a single, real human

nature behind the twisted masks of character, and justify the peremptory removal of those masks in the patients' best interest. Libido was Reich's revolutionary leverage, the promised manna that would be plentiful after the social and intrapsychic overthrow of the superego.

This conceptual sparring acquires concrete and far-reaching import when translated into clinical practice. From the beginning of his association with psychoanalysis Reich felt galled by the length of treatment, by the analyst's supposed neutrality and inconspicuousness, and by the patient's seemingly endless dodges and deceptions. What he wanted was to make the patient over into the free and open person that he, Reich, knew was trapped beneath the character armor. His Pygmalion impulse found its earliest outlet in a critique of Freudian method—a critique which was trenchant and shrewd, for Reich in his restlessness was able to see that the apparent compliance of patients was likely to be a pseudocompliance masking a continued hostility to the analysis. No one should suppose, however, that the Reich of *Character Analysis* (1933) was simply repairing a weakness in analytic procedure. Rather, he was revoking the whole Freudian therapeutic alliance and putting in its place a relationship more congenial to his hectoring disposition. Now the analyst would be a hero, daring to thwart the patient's resistances at every point, to take the full fury of his aggression, and then to crush his defensive system so that an ideal "genital character" could emerge.

Whatever the merits of this approach, it constituted a reversal of psychoanalytic ethics, whereby the therapist must try to refrain from passing judgment on the patient's conscious values. "Full orgastic potency" as Reich conceived it was not something his patients had hoped to attain when they came to him, but a distant ideal which *he* told *them* was the proper object of human striving, and which he regarded as beyond the reach of civilized man under capitalism. Only by joining

Reich's worldwide crusade could the patient hope to bring about the preconditions of complete mental health for himself and others. Submitting not just to the therapist's manipulations but to Reich's social vision as well, the patient was evidently meant to undergo a conversion experience and become a disciple—with or without "cure" in the conventional sense.

It is no secret, of course, that discipleship can be curative, offering as it does a resurgence of faith in a guiding parent figure and a meaningful life. As one case history may illustrate, the "religious" aspect of orgonomy is paramount for people who are not so much sick as confused and starved for purpose. In his book-length narrative of a Reichian treatment at the hands of Dr. Elsworth Baker, the actor Orson Bean patently accepts Reich as a savior. Bean never tells us what, if anything, was wrong with his biosystem before Dr. Baker began pushing and pedalling it, but he does say that simply by reading one of Reich's books he discovered the meaning of existence. For someone who has experienced one true orgasm, he then realized, "the question of what life is all about never has to be asked again." His own "messianic fervor" to convert others seems to have resulted chiefly from his empathy with the martyred leader. Reich, Bean tells us, was hounded by "the little character assassins of the world," who falsely accused him of having been a Communist and of pretending to cure cancer. In reality he was "one of the greatest men in the history of the human race." Thus, "Reich was one of the few true revolutionaries who ever lived and I had decided to join the revolution." Now filled with a Reichian sense of license, Bean and his new wife can "look up into the sky to see the little units of orgone energy tumbling and popping around in the atmosphere"; and he draws strength from knowing that those orgones "don't care about any of it, do they?" [14] He has become, as it were, homeopathically delusional, light-heartedly believing himself the beneficiary of special powers and therefore feeling lively enough to carry out ordinary Christian ideas about marriage and service in a fallen world.

When a therapy of total conversion produces such a benign outcome, we must give some credit to the convert's inherent stability. With less secure patients the effect may be altogether different. Bean himself remarks that the cracking of character armor causes severe "orgasm anxiety," an ultimate terror of letting go, and that "The only cure for it is to learn to tolerate it and hope that it will diminish" (Bean, p. 89). But suppose it doesn't diminish? "It is especially in the last phases of treatment," says Ola Raknes, "when the patient feels the orgonotic streamings as irresistible but dares not surrender to them, that the danger of suicide may be imminent and that all the skill of the therapist is needed to avert it" (Raknes, p. 125). One of Reich's own patients, Nic Waal, felt personally helped by the therapy but recalled that Reich's "cruel and penetrating technique" had tragic effects on some people, who "became either crushed or obsessively oppositional or projective . . ." [15] And Reich himself, in a temporarily recanting mood, confessed to Kurt Eissler in 1952 that the whole idea of trying to dissolve character

> is very dangerous. You see, the armor, thick as it is and as bad as it is, is a protective device, and it is good for the individual under present social and psychological circumstances to have it. He couldn't live otherwise. That is what I try to teach my doctors today. I tell them I am glad they don't succeed in breaking down that armor because people, who have grown up with such structures, are used to living with them. If you take that away, they break down. They can't, they just can't live any longer. . . . if you would break down all of the armoring in the world today, there would be chaos. Perfect chaos! Murder everywhere! (*RSF*, p. 110)

Even this negative statement, which has evidently had no deterrent effect on Reich's movement, clearly indicates that the scope of orgonomic treatment is nothing less than the removal of the individual's adaptive apparatus. That apparatus stands under indictment as the product of unwanted (i.e., societal) influences. Whether or not he retains his sanity, the patient will at least have been purged of evil. And what is sanity, after all? As Reich learned more of nature's secrets he began to value the wisdom of psychotics, whose ideas so amazingly resembled his own.[16] Without denying his original aim of securing orgastic potency, he came to treasure the emergence of the buried self in vatic form. Thus, in a halting and inconsistent way, Reich foreshadowed the fully inverted value system of his admirer R. D. Laing, who has decreed that "True sanity entails in one way or another the dissolution of the normal ego, that false self competently adjusted to our alienated social reality; the emergence of the 'inner' archetypal mediators of divine power, and through this death a rebirth, and the eventual re-establishment of a new kind of ego-functioning, the ego now being the servant of the divine, no longer its betrayer." [17]

We needn't be surprised, then, to learn that Reich's fanatically materialistic system gradually acquired all the superficial features of a religion. Orgonomy as finally elaborated possesses a pantheistic deity (the Cosmic Orgone Energy Ocean), a devil of sorts (Deadly Orgone Energy), an earthly heaven (the elusive but ever-beckoning perfect orgasm), a lost paradise (our matriarchal prehistory), an original sin (the imposition of patriarchy and sexual denial), a righteous animus toward evil (Reich's fulmination against every detumescent influence), and a body of disciples trained to evoke and bestow a holy substance that is invisible to unbelievers. And it has Reich himself explicitly playing Christ, a role he could not refuse after perceiving that the seemingly ascetic Jesus had been an ideal genital character who was crucified for anticipating orgonomy.[18] These parallels suggest, not that Reichianism is a religion, but that by virtue of its *contemptus mundi* it is structurally and rhetorically akin to one. Materialism such as Reich's elides into religious prophecy because its intent is to negate the Actual and make way for the Real, the suppressed inner kingdom.

No doubt a similar need for purgative negation informs all revolutionary dialectic, whatever its manifest goals; the more successful a movement is in pursuing those goals, the more easily the revolutionist can bury his negativity in practical work. What makes Reich a typical figure for our time is precisely the unmediated, insatiable quality of his apocalyptic drive, which finds nothing in reality to pause over for long. By casting himself as Christ, Reich at once confesses his worldly failure and makes a virtue of it, setting himself off from an ever wider conspiracy of persecutors who are blamed for his bad moods and lost opportunities. And paranoid though it may be, this strategy has a resonant effect on others who feel cheated by history, disillusioned with the customary radical mottoes, and therefore all the more goaded by iconoclastic passion.

It may be, indeed, that Reichianism chiefly provides its supporters with "scientific" validation of defenses against a loss of boundary between oneself and a menacing outer world. Sensations of emptiness and vulnerability flourish in an age when secure adversary identities (the revolutionist, the radical intellectual, the avant-garde artist) appear to be swallowed within an all-assimilating, all-cheapening sociopolitical system. The scarcity of recognizable *others*, whose differentness would permit a clear and purposeful self-definition on one's own part, may be an underrated factor contributing to modern anxiety. Norman Mailer felt it in the fifties when he was drawn toward Reichian energetics because he feared being "jailed in the prison air of other people's habits, other people's defeats, boredom, quiet desperation, and muted icy self-destroying rage" (*Advertisements*, p. 313),[19] and the same sensation is again common today, after the interlude of polarization and activism provided by the Vietnam war. Quite ordinary citizens as well as romantic anarchists now feel themselves to be rebuffed by standardized surroundings, enmeshed in automated procedures, assailed by motivational conditioning, awash in trivia, merged with their neighbors—and at a loss to know whom to blame or how the nets of dependency can be undone. Such a time is bound to be auspicious for purveyors of happiness, and doubly so for those who can stir up the old conviction that there is a simple battle to be won after all, a cause that lends historical consequence to one's own oppositional drive.

Although it may seem perverse to argue that a radically optimistic vision such as Reich's succeeds largely by mobilizing feelings of inadequacy and desperation, those feelings are just what we might expect to find undergirding any structure of manic affirmation. In Reich's case they are plainly apparent. The essence of orgonomy is that one's vital currents are always being either enhanced or drained away,[20] and that hence one can never be too careful about one's contacts. Despite his rhetoric of comradeship and cooperation, Reich can only be understood as sponsoring a jealous guarding of the self against a suspect world. Thus the ostensible aim of a loving mutuality is pursued through emphasis on one's own pelvic unblocking, one's own libido, one's own orgasm; and thus there is a hysterical urgency in Reich's proclamations that life need *not* be utterly oppressive, that children *can and must* break the death-grip of their parents, that heterosexual genitality *is* approachable despite society's concerted and sinister opposition to it. Reich's declaration that life energy is everywhere denies that it is nowhere. That denial was personally necessary to Reich, I gather, in order to abate his fear of being contaminated by others,[21] but it is also received as a blessing by people who, for good historical reasons, experience themselves as manipulated, depleted, and swept toward a paralytic apathy.

That the blessing is genuinely beneficial for most of those

who accept it cannot be doubted. The preponderant testimony of Reichian patients is that they have come to feel more at home with their bodies and more capable of useful action. Yet the prevalence in our society of Reichianism and related doctrines may be evidence of a reduced tolerance, in the dual sense of a diminished willingness to allow others to be themselves and a reduced capacity to withstand stress.

Whatever its successes, orgonomy is a therapy of imposition in which the patient's value system is forcibly assailed and replaced by the doctor's, which is presumed superior because it comes straight from the inspired teachings of Reich. Americans like to consider themselves resistant to such authoritarianism, but in a time of identity diffusion many people become at once more restive and more credulous, demanding that their minds be ravished by an infallible guru. Perhaps they stop short of commitment to overtly dictatorial schemes, such as Reich's proposal that anxiety-free sexuality be enforced by state decree.[22] But they are caught up by the general notion that freedom consists in the overthrow of customs, institutions, family ties, even the canons of scientific objectivity, all of which are thought to violate the supreme right of the inner self to find expression. Such a belief illustrates and hastens the shrinkage of horizons toward an anxious personal narcissism, with a consequent readiness to embrace any propositions that shore up that narcissism. A sense of exposure resulting in part from a loss of cultural sustenance causes the remaining fragments of tradition to be mistaken for the real source of unhappiness, and the process of deracination is then accelerated into a euphoric ideological program.

If this development is due in part to irreversible processes at work in the modern world, it is also traceable to an ethical assumption that can be consciously reconsidered. The assumption was originally Freud's, not Reich's: it was the belief, founded on positivistic nineteenth-century science, that "normal functioning" should be pursued as the highest end of ex-

istence. Once that belief leaves the hands of an ironic humanist like Freud, all conventional aspects of life, all bonds
between generations, all disciplines whose mastery requires
postponement of gratification can be made to appear as intolerable threats to somatic fulfillment. It is a short step, as we
have seen, from Freud's distinctly horrific conception of the
superego to Reich's decision that the superego must be
smashed. And it is just another step, one that happens to span
the arc of Reich's own career, to the compensatory idea of control over divine energies, for the new antagonism to "society"
requires that the self find its guardian in higher circles.

In the end, for Reich and many others who have tried to use
psychology as an all-sufficient ethical guide, the world can be
made safe for genitality only through cultic delusion, and perhaps not even then. Such examples ought to remind us that
man truly "functions normally" when his attention is directed
beyond his immediate well-being—when he is involved with
people and places, institutions and principles, that sustain
him even as they shape and limit him. To those who accept
this point at all, it is a truism; but it is one that casts a devas-
tating light on much romantic radicalism of the past quarter-
century.

Chapter Nine

REDUCTIONISM AND ITS DISCONTENTS

In some ways this most recent survey of the risks entailed in Freudian criticism may look like a return to the stance of Chapter One. Here, however, attention is given not only to problems within the practice of literary psychoanalysis, but also to the irreducibility of literature to any functional perspective. If my way of arguing, as usual, is somewhat negative, the purpose is affirmative: to renew appreciation of the criteria that enable rational, nonsectarian discourse about literature to occur.

*A*nyone who believes, as I do, that principles of Freudian psychoanalysis can be usefully applied to literary criticism must find himself repeatedly assailed by doubts: about the theory itself, about methodological pitfalls, above all about the weak and sometimes comical record of the Freudian critical tradition. The partisan of literary psychoanalysis is likely to be busier apologizing for that tradition than improving it with contributions of his own. And no matter how many scrupulous distinctions he may draw between responsible and "wild" uses of Freud, he can never quite dispel the suspicion that psychoanalysis is, as its opponents have always said, inherently reductionistic. The record all too clearly shows that a special danger of dogmatism, of clinical presumption, indeed of monomania, accompanies a method that purports to ferret out from literature a handful of previously known, perennially "deep" psychic concerns. It must be admitted that Freudian criticism too easily degenerates into a grotesque Easter-egg hunt: find the devouring mother, detect the inevitable castration anxiety, listen, between the syllables of verse, for the squeaking bedsprings of the primal scene. A critic who may have been drawn toward Freud by the promise of a heightened sensitivity to conflict in literature may, without ever knowing what has happened to him, become the purveyor of a peculiarly silly kind of allegory.

If some academic Freudians are slow to recognize the hazard of reductionism, it is not for lack of advice from their nonpsychoanalytic colleagues. On the contrary, a Freudian hears so much sermonizing against Freudian reductionism that he may come to regard that term as a provocation to battle. Secretly, in fact, he may even agree with his detractors that psychoanalysis "robs literature of its autonomy"—for that may be just what he wants it to do. Psychoanalytic criticism in its recent American phase has deliberately set itself apart from a certain mystique of literary autonomy, championed first in New-Critical formalism and later in the taxonomic theory of Northrop Frye. Rightly or wrongly, that theory has been attacked (by myself among others) as implicitly sponsoring an affect-stifling approach to literature. Insofar as the Freudian critic resents the "civilizing" claims that have been put forth in behalf of the academic literary curriculum, his worry about reductionism is going to be mitigated by a certain satisfaction he can take in brushing past formal or generic or ironic or (above all) morally uplifting aspects of literature and showing instead that even the sublimest masterpiece traffics in unconscious wishes. Though in practice most Freudian criticism is far from invigorating to read, its practitioner may feel that in writing it he is conjuring the Lawrentian dark gods and setting them loose on the "English" establishment.

Anyone who is not blinded by such vengeful intent, however, would have to grant that literature *is* autonomous in one important sense. However strenuous its birth pangs, a poem or novel exists independently of the emotions that went into it. Regarded autobiographically, it points back to those emotions; but in another light, the one cast by Eliot's notion of aesthetic impersonality, the work is what it is precisely by virtue of having put those emotions behind it. On temperamental grounds we may incline toward one critical attitude or the other, but on evidential grounds we have to acknowledge that a poem can mean many things besides the poet's psychomachia. A good part of its significance, furthermore, derives from its intricate relations with other poems—from its place in a tradition whose laws of development have very little to do with the psychic vicissitudes of individual poets.

Some guardians of literary autonomy would take this point

as a repudiation of all Freudian criticism, which they regard as reductionistic in its very essence. Psychoanalysis, they would say, is exactly a technique for making reductions from verbal manifestations to the psychic factors that supposedly determined those manifestations. If art is not mere behavior, wholly explainable by reference to the troubled minds that made it, then psychoanalytic criticism is always bound to falsify both the ontology and the multivalence of literature. What we want from criticism is not reduction to causes, but recognition of the inexhaustible and *irreducible* vitality that somehow inheres in the works themselves.

Expressed in such seemingly open-minded terms, the proscription against Freudian discourse sounds quite different from what it is, a denial of our right to pursue a certain range of problems. That psychoanalysis tends to treat a manifest text as an embodiment of psychic conflict cannot be doubted. But is this always and necessarily an unfruitful attitude for a critic to adopt? Authors do assuredly reveal wishes and anxieties when they write, and the experience of reading does have something to do with conflict management, if only in a simulated mode. Using psychoanalytic assumptions, a critic can show how a writer's public intention was evidently deflected by a private obsession. He can deal with blatant or subtle appeals to fantasy, as in the habitual practice of a genre like science fiction or the Gothic novel. He can reveal a hidden consistency behind shifts of tone or characterization, or make a new approach to a puzzle that has resisted commonsense solutions. Or again, he can draw biographical inferences on the basis of certain recurrent themes that the author hadn't consciously meant to display. Whatever its risks and deficiencies, Freudian reasoning has shown itself well adapted to such undertakings, which, though sternly denounced by purists, are established and useful critical enterprises.

In order to meet the real issue of reductionism without dismissing legitimate applications of psychoanalysis, it is necessary to realize that the mere proposing of a reductive idea doesn't in itself constitute reduction*ism*, the effective denial or denigration of all meanings but the reductive one that is being revealed. Reductive inferences are normal, though not equally prominent, in many schools of criticism. A critic is reducing— that is, diverting attention from the text to something that purportedly lies behind the text and helps to explain it— whenever he asserts that a work can be understood in relation to its author's social background or didactic intent or cultural allegiance, or even his literary tradition. Reductionism proper is a certain bigoted way of advancing such points, with the result that the work in its singularity is sacrificed to the interpretive scheme instead of being illuminated by it.

Thus it is reductive, but possibly quite justifiable and helpful, to maintain that a common current of homosexual feeling for "the Handsome Sailor" runs between Claggart and Vere in *Billy Budd;* although the point might not originally occur to anyone but a Freudian, he could show other readers that his reduction makes sense of otherwise obscure features of the text. If the same critic were to say or imply that homosexuality is "the meaning" of *Billy Budd,* he would be not only reductive but reductionistic as well. Or again, to cite a recent example, when Michael West argues a connection in Thoreau's writings between excremental imagery, punning, distaste for women, contempt for philanthropic sympathy, and fear of tuberculosis, he is making reductions that would have been unthinkable before Freud.[1] Yet West's article is not in my opinion reductionistic, for *Walden* in his hands, instead of dwindling to an illustration of theory, becomes richer and stranger than ever.

The fact remains, however, that the greater part of Freudian criticism is not just reductive, as it is bound to be, but reductionistic as well, and to a degree unmatched in any other school. When we ask why this should be the case, we find the answer immediately in the root assumptions of Freudian metapsychology. I have in mind the axioms that all psychic events are determined; that the deterministic chain originates in biological drives whose frustration and deflection eventuate in mental structures, ideas, and sublimated aims; and that the infantile and the prior therefore explain the adult and the contemporary. These notions together yield a picture of man as a creature chiefly occupied with fending off disturbing stimuli, both from his own soma and from external sources of disequilibrium. Alienated from his instinctive needs, absorbed in trying to appease a superego which has been precipitated from parental taboos, this rather sneaky fellow is conceived as being always on the lookout for ways to bootleg a little gratification, to give sway to the eternal baby within. And this narcissistic project, however petty and ridiculous it may appear to the uninitiated, is considered the quintessentially human activity, for man is above all the animal who turns against himself and then chafes against his self-inflicted unhappiness. Thus, no matter what action or text is being examined, the essentials of metapsychology dictate a mode of analysis in which persistent infantile factors will be stressed at the expense of nonconflictual ones—cognitive, conventional, formal, or ethical.

When man creates art, psychoanalysis disposes us to view that art as the product of a provisional unburdening, and to regard a work's meaning as coextensive with the thoughts or fantasies that were discharged in the act of composition. Hence the inevitable biographical orientation of all Freudian critics who haven't explicitly pledged to leave authors' minds out of account. However variously they may draw up the ground rules of criticism, psychoanalytic commentators tend to agree in taking a poem to be a need-satisfying, as opposed to a meaning-generating, device. Their one concession to multivalence is the idea of overdetermination—a principle which, as the name implies, allows several needs to be met by a single expression but does not depart from the basic Freudian orientation to conflict settlement. Interpretation, in short, remains a question of building bridges between the poem and the psy-chic conditions from which it arose, and of which it must be a manifestation. The fact that other people besides the artist respond to the poem is taken to indicate, not that a symptoma-tic interpretation is uncalled for, but that it can be applied to both parties in the transaction: author and reader are thought to communicate only in the sense that they both take the same words as their pretext for assuaging the tension with which they must continually live.

The narrowness of vision resulting from such assumptions is apparent even in highly refined statements of Freudian liter-ary theory, the most imposing of which remains Norman N. Holland's *The Dynamics of Literary Response.* No Freudian has taken greater pains to make psychoanalysis accountable for subtle differences of genre and effect, and none has shown greater diffidence about armchair diagnosis of authors. Yet the rules set forth in the *Dynamics,* if followed to the letter, could hardly fail to result in reductionist criticism. For Holland as-serts, merely on the basis of an extrapolation from the Freu-dian approach to dreams and jokes, that one infantile fantasy lies at the origin and heart of each literary work. Although he makes gestures of coexistence toward many styles of criticism, Holland nevertheless declares that "the psychoanalytic mean-ing underlies all the others" [2]—a fact which can be announced in advance of any given instance, since, in Holland's view, the true purpose of even the most artifice-laden work is to enable a "core fantasy" to manifest itself in a respectable disguise. Holland even provides us with a "dictionary" of such fan-tasies—each pertaining to one of the classic erogenous zones and modes of gratification—in the certainty that he is cata-loguing the very wellsprings of literary expression.

Holland is correct in believing that no one but a Freudian critic will be able to arrive at a work's "underlying meaning" in his sense of the term. What he does not realize, or hadn't yet realized in 1968, is that this is a handicap rather than an advantage. The handicap is at once social and intellectual, for the critic following Holland's lead can have no hope of gaining wide agreement to his readings and no opportunity to be chastened by reasonable objections from the unanalyzed, whose resistance is predicted and discounted by the theory. Above all, the critic will have locked himself into a rigid set of procedures: stripping each work to its supposed core and then presenting its other thematic and formal aspects as so many defensive strategies, whether or not they are experienced as defensive in the act of reading. Such overcommitment to a method prior to examining a given work can only diminish the critic's receptiveness and adaptability, meanwhile leaving the disagreeable, and finally incredible, impression that great literature is merely a subterfuge for venting such forbidden thoughts as "if I am phallically aggressive and do not submit to my mother, she will castrate me." [3]

Although Holland's theory of literature is not the only one that might be drawn up from Freudian premises, it is disturbingly loyal to those premises—so much so that we must ask whether a full-scale commitment to psychoanalysis can make a critic anything *but* a reductionist. Here, however, I must attend to a strong objection from advocates of modern psychoanalysis. They would remind me that Freud's narrow determinism, with its exclusively male perspective, its overrating of the Oedipus complex, its neglect of interpersonal as opposed to intrapsychic dynamics, and its billiard-ball notion of cause and effect, has long been superseded within the psychoanalytic tradition. (In fact, I have previously been taken to task in print for using the very adjective "Freudian," which is thought to lend the movement an unnecessarily quaint air.) It is the psychoanalysts themselves, after all, who now warn against reductionist interpretation in the form of "originology," the automatic ascribing of determinative significance to infantile factors. Can't we, instead of appealing to nebulous and suspect ideas of critical sensibility, find a remedy for reductionism *within* contemporary psychoanalysis?

The hope for such a remedy rests with what is loosely called ego psychology: the totality of post-Freudian developments stressing the adaptive and integrative capacities of the mind. I refer to such theorists as Anna Freud, Heinz Hartmann, Rudolf Loewenstein, Ernst Kris, Robert Waelder, David Rapaport, and Erik Erikson.[4] In different degrees all these analysts recognize that Freud's psychic model exaggerates the individual's helplessness to govern his life. All seek to loosen the strict determinism of infantile trauma and to deny or mitigate Freud's antithesis between libidinal impulse and the forces of civilization. By and large, the ego psychologists retain Freud's interest in drives and their derivatives, but by invoking such concepts as identity, neutralized energy, multiple function, and the conflict-free sphere of the ego, they try to make room within the Freudian system for an acknowledgment that the mind is not exclusively concerned with combating anxiety.

These developments, however, though they have certainly rendered psychoanalysis less dogmatic, do not seem to me to constitute a reliable antidote to reductionism. Most ego psychologists, despite their awareness that all-purpose explanatory universals really explain nothing, are scarcely more prepared than Freud himself was to acknowledge the prospective (not regressive) and meaning-creating (not confessional) aspects of art. Indeed, it would not be altogether perverse to suggest that ego psychology makes the problem of reductionism harder to recognize and address. The very sophistication of recent doctrine may allow its spokesman to forget what Freud usually remembered, that the secret of artistic genius is beyond his science. A theory like Ernst Kris's, which depicts creativity as playfully controlled regression, comes just near enough to accommodating artistic freedom to convince the critic that he can put reductionism behind him and deal with art in all its fullness. In actuality he is still bound to a largely passive and defensive conception of mind—one that omits or minimizes exactly that drive toward perfection of form that distinguishes the artist from the ordinary neurotic.

The ego psychologists' regard for a wide variety of social and historical factors unquestionably marks an advance over Freud's unvarying emphasis on the universal Oedipus complex. Again, however, we must ask whether the multiplying of considered determinants overcomes, or merely complicates, the functionalistic habit of interpretation. Isn't literature still being treated as a vector of the influences that attended its composition? And aren't some influences still being given an arbitrary precedence over others? The recent scholarly fashion of psychohistory, which has not yet had much impact on literary studies, provides some distressing examples of what happens when a commentator increases the number of potential determinants without relinquishing the priority afforded to infantile ones: the result is simply to widen the range of phenomena he thinks he has accounted for in classic Freudian terms. Ego psychology as we see it in, say, Erikson's writings is profoundly ambiguous, pointing simultaneously toward and away from the early crises of libidinal life. Such ambiguity does afford the ego psychologist some room in which to follow the promptings of common sense. Too often, however, ego psychology amounts to little more than a shift of mood or ideology on the critic's part, enabling him to give a positive, upbeat emphasis to the same data that used to be taken as signs of neurosis.[5]

This scarcity of firm propositional content may help to explain why, in literary studies, "ego psychology" has been frequently invoked but almost never satisfactorily illustrated. Psychoanalytic reviewers, finding that psychoanalytic critics are still unearthing "id-psychological" infantile fantasies, regularly accuse those critics of not having incorporated the insights of ego psychology into their method. The implication is that the reviewers themselves do better in their own criticism, but this—to judge from the daisy chain of chiding reviews—is rarely the case. Each critic apparently hopes that by analyzing fantasy content he will be manifesting the adaptive and integrative power of the authorial ego that managed to put all this primitive material to aesthetic use. But since psychoanalysis offers no means of studying the transcendence of conflict, there is no way the critic can discuss that power without interrupting himself. Even if he pauses to toss off some handsome compliments to the author's flexibility before returning to the nitty-gritty of unconscious themes, those themes in all their rawness will probably govern the tone of his criticism. And if they don't—if the critic successfully represents his author as having reconciled multiple pressures on his equanimity—he may still be writing reductionistically, for reductionism comes precisely from the illusion that one has said all that bears saying.

There are, to be sure, some currents within ego psychology that look exceptionally salutary for the psychoanalytic critic who is as mindful of fallacies as of phalluses. Thus the post-Kleinian British theorists of "object-relations," such as W. R. D. Fairbairn, Edith Jacobson, and D. W. Winnicott, have been deservedly cited as fostering a subtle and constructive view of literature.[6] In studying childhood these writers depart from the standard account of incestuous and patricidal conflict and offer instead a detailed picture of the child's efforts to survive the loss of maternal symbiosis—a project that predates sexual roles and continues beyond the so-called passing of the Oedipus complex. By focusing less on drives and defenses than on ego-stabilizing feats of introjection, the post-Kleinians succeed in connecting the terms of Freud's intrapsychic model to the real human figures—parents and their surrogates—who impinge on a subject's formation of identity. In consequence, a critic following their lead can consider works of art, not as symptomatic expressions, but as "transitional objects"—that is, as productions that both reconstitute a destroyed inner world and enact a new competence and a new mode of relatedness to the forbidding outer world. And this view in turn restores to literature some of the dignity it lost when Freud conceived of the writer as escaping from reality to self-aggrandizing fantasy. Now the artistic process appears as a special version of the way "reality" is continually constituted by each mind as it attunes itself to objects of longing and rage.

These are welcome potentialities, but they leave the problem of reductionism unresolved. A post-Kleinian is as likely as a Freudian to see a literary work not as an independent aesthetic structure but as a product of the forces that happen to interest him. When art is analogized to the "transitional" teddy bear instead of to the dream, it is still being treated as something other than itself, and its biographical genesis is still favored over its public import. The shifting of explanatory focus to an earlier stage of childhood, and from mechanisms of repression and displacement to those of projection and introjection, makes for a new set of insights but not for relief from the translating of literature into the preexisting terms of a system. And the system, again, is one whose orientation to need fulfillment leaves little room for appreciating the abundance and extravagance, the sheer surplus of invention, to be found in, say, a Shakespeare or a Dickens. The essential fact is inescapable: methodological provisos alone cannot ensure that a reductive style of interpretation won't result in reductionistic criticism.

If, despite all recent complications, psychoanalytic hermeneutics still give greatest weight to infantile themes, we must recognize that the method itself blocks the path of a critic who would avoid reductionism. For that method is at once reductive in impulse and uniquely minute in focus, entangling its user in line-by-line decodings that other readers may regard as entirely mad. (Marxist criticism, for instance, is just as zealous for explanation, but having no fondness for infancy and no technique for breaking statements into their alleged hidden components, it tends to come up with global formulations that can be accepted or shrugged off without much violence to our sense of what a given poem or novel contains.) To be a nonreductionist Freudian requires an extraordinary detachment from the very assumptions that allow one to perceive unconscious themes in the first place.

It is little wonder that few psychoanalytic critics are willing to endure the vertigo that accompanies such self-division. The alternative, however, is not simply dogmatism but—if the critic has an inkling of his plight—a special bewilderment that stems from prolonged reductive practice. A conscientious Freudian is bound to begin wondering, sooner or later, whether his conclusions say more about the text under discussion or about his own temperament. Here he is ill served by the notoriously compliant rules of exegesis that psychoanalysis has provided him. The very ease with which one critic can diagnose Keats's orality, and another Ben Jonson's anality, must leave each of them with the haunting fear that he has been taking those authors' works as projective ink blots and composing, not literary criticism, but cryptic fragments of a libidinal autobiography. When the critic appeals to the guidance of ego psychology, he gets only further cause for worry: if that school tells him anything at all, it is that minds, including his own, necessarily indulge in just such imperious misapprehensions in the interest of imposing a bearable stamp upon experience. The farther he gets beyond the provincial this-equals-that symbology of early psychoanalysis, the more vulnerable the critic becomes to misgivings about the rationale of his work. Now he may suspect, not simply that he has been a reductionist, but that his reductionistic statements have had himself as their secret object.

Some such realization appears to have struck Norman Holland, whose most recent pronouncements shed a new and surprising light on the whole question of Freudian reductionism.[7] Holland, tacitly abandoning the mechanical fantasy-defense model of mental activity that underlay *The Dynamics of Literary Response,* has simultaneously made his peace with ego psychology and tried to face up to the shaky philosophical status of psychoanalytic interpretations. The two developments are intimately bound together. As soon as Holland replaces the search for a work's "core fantasy" with an ego-psychological search for its "identity theme"—that is, for the unalterable style of being-in-the-world that characterizes the work's author—he finds himself paralyzed by the thought that he too, as a critic, has an identity theme which is warping all his perceptions.[8] The old Freudian exercise of compensating for one's bias, Holland decides, is futile, for even the most skeptical critic is exercising his identity in the very act of trying to neutralize it. Which is to say, in my terms, that psychoanalytic critics along with all others have been reductionists in a hitherto unsuspected sense: they have reduced literature to the rigid and narrow outlines of their own personalities.

Less sanguine Freudians than Holland, arriving at this evident impasse, might infer that their method must have been faulty from the start, or perhaps that life is too short to be squandered on such a chancy vocation as literary criticism. But if all critics, and not just psychoanalytic ones, write projectively, perhaps a Freudian can use his special insight to mark the way toward a new candor. The proper subject matter of criticism, Holland now sees, is not literary works at all, but the critic's private digestion of those works, whose actual properties, if any, can never be grasped.[9] Let us (says Holland) continue being critics and redouble our study of psychoanalysis, but let us also purify our discourse of old-fashioned predications about the content of books. We Freudians, specifically, should henceforth eschew such statements as "the poem transforms this fantasy into that meaning" and "The poem strikes a good balance between fantasy and defense" and confine ourselves instead to such statements as "Here are my associations to the poem" and "For me the poem seems to hang together." Although Holland doesn't offer this proposal as a retreat from reductionism—indeed, he doesn't grant that his earlier scheme raised that problem—we cannot fail to notice that the curse of reductionism is being summarily lifted here, along with every other liability that attends the making of definite statements about literature.

Whether or not Holland's new reasoning is sound, it does inspire a utilitarian question: who will want to read the confessional criticism he now advocates? Why, if we must forgo criticism's traditional goal of making empirically adequate remarks about texts, should we take an interest in one another's ruminations about "how it feels to me"? The doubt is made more urgent by Holland's way of expounding his position. In his soon-to-be-published book *Five Readers Reading,* he exhaustively analyzes the responses to certain pieces of literature by anonymous college students known to us as Sandra, Seymour, Samantha, *et al.,* who are variously reminded, when they read a certain poem, of a telephone call from home, a case of sunburn, and a judgment that the Pacific Ocean is placid. Granted, these revelations are not offered for their intrinsic value but as proof that the student readers are in some sense not apprehending the same poem.[10] Yet Sandra and Seymour cannot help but impress us as disquieting harbingers of the new personal criticism recommended by Holland.

I for one would expect Holland's meditation in the presence of a poem to be more enlightening than Seymour's. All the same, I might become fatigued after a while by Holland's protestations that I needn't suppose *his* thoughts to apply to *my* perceived poem, as if I couldn't notice the differences without his help. Furthermore, and more fundamentally, Holland seems to me to be forgetting the entire raison d'être of critical activity. We don't go to criticism to discover Seymour's identity theme, or Holland's, or Frank Kermode's, or anyone else's. We go to criticism because we hope to learn more about literature than we could have figured out for ourselves. A critic who rejects that hope on philosophical principle, while nevertheless urging us to adopt an interpretive apparatus which is now guaranteed to yield no results, can only be regarded as conducting a highly unusual going-out-of-business sale.

But what about Holland's epistemological challenge? Isn't it the case that we can only know our own subjective construction of the world? And if so, mustn't we literary critics admit that our only basis of communication is to take turns displaying how we have each assimilated a poem to our private needs? Perhaps we *are* all incurable reductionists who have no means of mediating the inconsistencies between our readings.

This pessimism indeed follows from the tradition of epistemology in which Freudianism squarely resides—the "school of suspicion," as Paul Ricoeur has aptly named it— which mounts a merciless critique of other people's social or psychic bias while holding out the prospect that the individual demystifier, armed with a special technique of self-correction, can get at the truth on his own.[11] When that individual eventually begins to doubt his own objectivity, he typically becomes stranded, as Holland now is, with the feeling that knowledge is altogether chimerical; and then his one solace is that he has dared to look farther into the abyss than those simple Cartesians who still think they can make statements about objects—for example, about poems. All this chagrin, however, rests on a fundamental mistake about the basis of knowledge. Knowledge is a social project, not a personal one. It has nothing to do with the individual investigator's efforts to purge himself of unconscious bias, and everything to do with shared principles of validation. In Karl Popper's philosophy of science, for example, adequate (though not provably true) statements are considered possible thanks to a friendly-hostile social effort to falsify those statements according to agreed-upon empirical criteria; and Popper, as it happens, devotes some scathing pages to the claim of Freudians, among other self-analyzers, to possess unique insight and hence a special insurance against error.[12] Although knowledge of a poem is admittedly more problematic than knowledge of, say, a molecule, in each instance the hope of approximating that knowledge rests with a community of people who can be counted on to reject patently wrong ideas and eventually to prefer relatively accurate and useful ones. They can be counted on, that is to say, provided their concern for distinguishing between plausible and frivolous statements hasn't been eroded by a commitment to subjectivism.

Subjectivism, however, is in the air, and not just among captive freshmen who want to escape judgment by declaring each reading to be as valid as every other. As I indicated at the outset, American psychoanalytic criticism has drawn some of its energy from a wish to rescue literature in all its affectual intensity from the classifying and formalizing academicians, the high priests of objectivity. In announcing that no reader perceives the poem except as an extension of his ego, Holland withdraws the much-resisted "elitist" implication that some people are more careful readers than others; and this remission then permits all readers to trade associations to the poem on a relaxed and equal basis. As one of Holland's supporters remarks of the new attitude, "This in-mixing of self and other makes interpretation a potentially private affair, but it also can lead to a more inclusive sharing of emotional as well as intellectual dynamics than is now available." [13] Don't we have here the ethos of "encounter," with a trading of isolated acts of introspection ("shared dynamics") replacing a concern for the object under discussion?

I know from my own experience in psychoanalytic seminars that a poem or story can trigger highly intuitive responses of the sort that Holland wants to make central to criticism. Some of the most exhilarating moments in my teaching have come when, during a pooling of free speculations about unconscious themes in a piece of literature, a sentiment of adventure and catharsis has swept across the classroom without anyone's being able to state what the apparent consensus was. Of course there wasn't any consensus; we were merely allowing one another a license to fantasize aloud in the aftermath of reading. I myself have hoped, as Holland's school does, that some of that subliminal excitement, that sense of having one's feelings brought into sudden and total coherence, could be carried directly into critical discourse. The hope, however, is illusory. For shared dynamics, as Sandra and Seymour remind us, lose a good deal in transposition to print, and readers of criticism will not be persuaded to accept their remnants in lieu of reasonable statements about literature. Whatever excitement criticism can generate must rest with the force and justice of those statements—must rest, in other words, with a propositional risk-taking that Holland now explicitly abjures.

Holland's new position may stand as an extreme example of the attempt to keep following psychoanalytic procedures regardless of the cost—to solve the problem of reductionism, not by adopting a broader outlook than that of psychoanalytic functionalism, but by ceasing to claim that one's reductive ideas are valid for other readers. My own preference is the more ordinary one of assuming that critics and their readers are apprehending approximately the same poem; of trying to narrow the differences of perception that do exist; and of coping with reductionism by explicitly recognizing Freudian inferences *as* reductions that will have to justify themselves on evidential grounds. If a critic remembers that psychoanalysis reduces as a matter of course, he may contrive ways of either using the method sparingly for limited ends or, if more ambitiously, then at least with cognizance of the factors that are automatically being excluded from his argument.

A critic who wants to avail himself of psychoanalysis would be well advised not only to seek out the most defensible and unmechanistic concepts within the system but also to think unsparingly about what is provincial and intolerant in that system. If he understands that Freudian reasoning ascribes key significance to its favorite themes, and that its supple rules of interpretation make the discovery of those themes a foregone conclusion; if he sees that the method tends to dichotomize between manifest and latent content even when the border between them is undiscernible; if he knows that psychoanalysis can say nothing substantial about considerations that fall outside an economics of desire and defense; and if he admits that it has a natural penchant for debunking—for sniffing out erotic and aggressive fantasies in the "purest" works and for mocking all pretensions to freedom from conflict—the critic may be able to borrow the clinical outlook without losing his intellectual independence and sense of proportion. He could hardly be blamed if, after weighing all these hazards, he decided to exchange Freud for, say, Fredson Bowers. But if not—if he recognized that Freud in his often questionable manner grasped some essential truths about motivation—he would at least see his rhetorical task in a clear light. He would realize, that is, that in order to communicate with other readers he must look past psychoanalysis and establish a common ground of literary perception.

This counsel, I know, downgrades Freudian criticism in the orthodox sense of rendering texts into psychoanalese, as if they were just so many illustrations of clinical patterns. But that criticism has always violated the spirit of Freud's writings, which, though sometimes reckless and confused, were never simply the consequence of "applying the method" to new materials. Freud was forever testing his ideas, looking for the edges of their scope and drawing back in deference to the unknown or the inexplicable. In a word, Freud was not a doctrinaire Freudian; he was a man provisionally taking a reductive posture toward phenomena in order to find whether anything plausible and important might be learned that way. The nearest equivalent in literary criticism wouldn't be a consistent psychoanalytic reading of an author's works, but a book like Harold Bloom's *The Anxiety of Influence*, which, for all its arch mannerisms, emulates Freud at his most inquisitive: the

Freud, I mean, who set aside cultural piety in order to look for psychic lawfulness where people would least have expected to find it.[14]

The fact that a critic's thesis is reductive—for example, Bloom's thesis that a poet's real business is to render his predecessors less intimidating by misrepresenting them as mere forerunners of himself—is no reason to reject it out of hand. The question must always be whether we are better or worse readers for having attended to the critic's argument. By that criterion even an argument that oversteps itself at certain points may earn the right to be remembered. We owe more, after all, to an Empson or a Burke—both of them indebted to Freud's example but unbound by his "methodology"—than to dozens of exegetes who have never once strayed onto the forbidden ground of the extraliterary. Though Empson and Burke and Bloom all make reductions, none of them is to a significant degree a reductionist. For their reductions, however startling and even outrageous, are put forward *as* reductions, as intellectual thrusts that needn't be confounded with the essence or value of the literature being scrutinized. These critics constantly imply a humility before the poems which, with seeming arrogance, they are temporarily turning inside out.

The present disarray of psychoanalytic criticism is no doubt a cause for satisfaction among people who never cared for "deep" interpretation and who now feel confirmed in their resolution to allow literature to speak for itself. The only way to do that, however, is to remain silent—a sacrifice beyond the saintliest critic's power. To be a critic is precisely to take a stance different from the author's and to pursue a thesis of one's own. Among the arguments it is possible to make, reductive ones are without doubt the trickiest, promising Faustian knowledge but often misrepresenting the object of inquiry and deluding the critic into thinking he has cracked the author's code. To forswear all reductions, however, is not the answer: that is the path of phobia. A critic can avoid reductionism, yet still give his intellect free rein, only by keeping his skepticism in working order. If psychoanalysis, originally the most distrustful of psychologies, has by its worldly success and conceptual elaboration become a positive impediment to skepticism, we need be no more surprised than Freud himself would have been at such all-too-human backsliding. A critic's sense of limits, like Freud's own, must come not from the fixed verities of a doctrine but from his awe at how little he can explain. And that awe in turn must derive from his openness to literature—from his sense that the reader in him, happily, will never be fully satisfied by what the critic in him has to say.

NOTES

Chapter One

1. For a schematic analysis of the present status of psychoanalysis, see Gardner Murphy, "The Current Impact of Freud on American Psychology," *Freud and the Twentieth Century*, ed. Benjamin Nelson (New York, 1957), pp. 102–122.

2. This fact may be attributable to the lack of allowance for dynamic factors in Gestalt psychology, coupled with an exclusion of thematic considerations, a tendency to elevate "good Gestalt" (whole form) into a criterion of excellence, and an incapacity to deal with the cumulative and reflective sense of form involved in reading. But see Herbert J. Muller, *Science and Criticism: The Humanistic Tradition in Contemporary Thought* (New Haven, 1943), pp. 157–167; H. E. Rees, *A Psychology of Artistic Creation as Evidenced in Autobiographical Statements of Artists* (New York, 1942); Werner Wolff, *The Expression of Personality: Experimental Depth Psychology* (New York, 1943); and E. H. Gombrich, *Art and Illusion: A Study in the Psychology of Pictorial Representation* (New York, 1960). For a psychoanalytic critique of Gestalt art theory see Anton Ehrenzweig, *The Psycho-Analysis of Artistic Vision and Hearing* (London, 1953). Recent evidence that "active perception" psychology may illuminate literary form is offered by Morse Peckham in *Man's Rage for Chaos; Biology, Behavior, and the Arts* (Philadelphia, 1965).

3. *Freud: The Mind of the Moralist* (New York, 1959), p. 121.

4. *A General Introduction to Psychoanalysis,* tr. Joan Riviere (New York, 1960), p. 384.

5. For Freud's Romanticism see Rieff, pp. 204–219, 345 f., and Ernest Jones, *The Life and Work of Sigmund Freud*, 3 vols. (New York, 1953–57), I, 28–30. For his reflection of both artistic and bourgeois ideals see Lionel Trilling, "Art and Neurosis," *The Liberal Imagination: Essays on Literature and Society* (Garden City, N.Y., 1953), pp.

159–178, and Norman N. Holland, *Psychoanalysis and Shakespeare* (New York, Toronto, London, 1966), pp. 9–44.

6. See E. Pumpian-Mindlin, ed., *Psychoanalysis as Science: The Dixon Lectures on the Scientific Status of Psychoanalysis* (Stanford, 1952). Recent years have seen a certain rapprochement between those psychoanalysts who are sensitive to empirical criticism and those academic psychologists who are weary of the stimulus-response rat race. One promising meeting ground is the building of conceptual models that combine mental processes which have been experimentally verified in piecemeal form. See especially Gerald S. Blum, *A Model of the Mind: Explored by Hypnotically Controlled Experiments and Examined for its Psychodynamic Implications* (New York and London, 1961), and Silvan S. Tomkins and Samuel Messick, eds., *Computer Simulation of Personality: Frontier of Psychological Theory* (New York and London, 1963).

7. For a defense of the role of metaphors in science see Abraham Kaplan, *The Conduct of Inquiry: Methodology for Behavioral Science* (San Francisco, 1964).

8. I am referring not only to Freud's late, much-criticized reduction of all instincts to Eros and Death, but also to his hydraulic account of quantities of libido. One group of adaptational psychologists, for example, holds that "It is irrelevant to our clinical understanding to posit an energy whose existence can never be demonstrated for behavior which is meaningful only in terms of motivation, psychologic mechanism, and ultimate action"—that is, in the other terms of psychoanalysis. See Abram Kardiner, Aaron Karush, and Lionel Ovessey, "A Methodological Study of Freudian Theory," *Journal of Nervous and Mental Disease,* 79 (July–October 1959), 11–19, 133–143, 207–221, 341–356. Other cogent attacks on Freudian neurophysiology, delivered from a standpoint of sympathy toward the behavioral observations of psychoanalysis, may be found in Norman S. Greenfield and William C. Lewis, eds., *Psychoanalysis and Current Biological Thought* (Madison and Milwaukee, Wis., 1965).

9. Significant critiques of the higher-level abstractions of psychoanalysis may be found in Heinz Hartmann, Ernst Kris, and Rudolph M. Loewenstein, "Comments on the Formation of Psychic Structure," *The Psychoanalytic Study of the Child,* 2 (1946), 11–37; Kenneth Mark Colby, *Energy and Structure in Psychoanalysis* (New York, 1955); David Rapaport, *The Structure of Psychoanalytic Theory* (New York, 1960); Peter Madison, *Freud's Concept of Repression and Defense* (Minneapolis, Minn., 1961); and Merton M. Gill, *Topography and*

Systems in Psychoanalytic Theory (New York, 1963). Regrettably, the preponderance of clinical and theoretical writing shows that such clarifications have been unheeded.

10. *Freud or Jung* (London, 1950), p. 165.

11. See Freud, *A General Introduction to Psychoanalysis* (New York, 1920), *New Introductory Lectures on Psycho-Analysis* (New York, 1933), and *An Outline of Psychoanalysis* (London, 1939). The first work takes fullest account of the skeptical reader's doubts, but lacks reference to Freud's important concept of the superego. Charles Brenner's *An Elementary Textbook of Psychoanalysis* (New York, 1955) repairs this and other omissions. However far the student continues his reading, he should not overlook Freud's early master-piece, *The Interpretation of Dreams* (1900; James Strachey's transla-tion of 1953 is now a paperback, New York, 1965). Useful surveys of the movement's bewildering history are Ruth L. Munroe, *Schools of Psychoanalytic Thought: An Exposition, Critique, and Attempt at In-tegration* (New York, 1955), and J. A. C. Brown, *Freud and the Post-Freudians* (London, 1961). Edward Glover's *Freud or Jung* (London, 1950), while hardly impartial, is indispensable for an under-standing of the logical incompatibility of two systems which liter-ary people sometimes tolerantly blend. Among the numerous books about Freud himself, Philip Rieff's *Freud: The Mind of the Moralist* (New York, 1959) is perhaps the most helpful in placing psychoanalysis in the context of the intellectual and scientific his-tory and the ethical assumptions from which it emerged. See also Ernest Jones's biography, cited above, n. 6.

12. *An Autobiographical Study* (London, 1948), p. 119.

13. "Freud and Literature," *The Liberal Imagination*, p. 60.

14. See Glover, pp. 185 f.; Louis Fraiberg, "Psychology and the Writer: The Creative Process," *Literature and Psychology*, 5 (Novem-ber 1955), 72–77, and "New Views of Art and the Creative Process in Psychoanalytic Ego Psychology," *Literature and Psychology*, 11 (Spring 1961), 45–55; Ernst Kris, *Psychoanalytic Explorations in Art* (London, 1953), pp. 13–63; and Lawrence S. Kubie, *Neurotic Distor-tion of the Creative Process* (Lawrence, Kan., 1958), passim.

15. See, for example, Erich Neumann, *Art and the Creative Uncon-scious* (London, 1959). Neumann's attack on the "personalistic" ap-proach enables him to argue that art communicates "numinous" archetypal powers which "are eternal, and . . . touch upon the eternal existence of man and the world" (p. 129). This is not psy-chology but Neo-Platonism—a fact that becomes especially clear

when Neumann praises Beethoven for "a break-through into the realm of essence" (p. 103). For a defense of the Jungian position, however, see Morris Philipson, *Outline of a Jungian Aesthetics* (Evanston, Ill., 1963). The outstanding Jungian contribution to criticism (its references to Freud are merely courteous, not eclectic) is Maud Bodkin, *Archetypal Patterns in Poetry: Psychological Studies of Imagination* (London, 1934). See also Jolande Jacobi, *Complex / Archetype / Symbol*, tr. Ralph Manheim (New York, 1959).

16. See, however, William Phillips' judicious caution against using terms like "neurotic" and "healthy" to characterize works of art. *Art and Psychoanalysis*, ed. William Phillips (Cleveland and New York, 1963), "Introduction: Art and Neurosis," pp. xii–xxiv.

17. *Psychoanalytic Explorations in Art*, p. 15.

18. Representative examples of the recent interest in the psychology of genres and movements are F. L. Lucas, *Literature and Psychology* (London, 1951), Ernst Kris, *Psychoanalytic Explorations in Art* (London, 1953), Simon O. Lesser, *Fiction and the Unconscious* (Boston, 1957), William Wasserstrom, *Sex and Sentiment in the Genteel Tradition* (Minneapolis, Minn., 1959), Leslie A. Fiedler, *Love and Death in the American Novel* (New York, 1960, 1966), Irving Malin, *New American Gothic* (Carbondale, Ill., 1962), and Angus Fletcher, *Allegory: The Theory of a Symbolic Mode* (Ithaca, N.Y., 1964). For psychoanalytic approaches to history itself see Erik H. Erikson, *Young Man Luther: A Study in Psychoanalysis and History* (New York, 1958), Norman O. Brown, *Life Against Death: The Psychoanalytical Meaning of History* (Middletown, Conn., 1959), and Bruce Mazlish, ed., *Psychoanalysis and History* (Englewood Cliffs, New Jersey, 1963). Erikson's work in particular is an eloquent refutation of the opinion that psychoanalytic premises necessarily make for a reductive view of events (including literary events) which demand interpretation on several levels.

19. *Counter-Statement* (Los Altos, Calif., 1953), p. 124. For a more rigorously psychoanalytic exposition of the same idea, see Appendix I of the second edition of Frederick J. Hoffman's *Freudianism and the Literary Mind* (Baton Rouge, La., 1957).

20. *Fiction and the Unconscious* (New York, 1962), pp. 121–187.

21. See *Leonardo da Vinci and a Memory of His Childhood*, tr. James Strachey (New York, 1964), and "Dostoevsky and Parricide," *Collected Papers*, 5 vols. (New York, 1959), V, 222–242.

22. For a defense of this new attitude see Norman N. Holland, *Psychoanalysis and Shakespeare* (New York, 1966), pp. 293–349.

23. See, however, his indulgent *Delusion and Dream: An Interpretation*

in the Light of Psychoanalysis of Gradiva, a Novel, *by Wilhelm Jensen,* tr. Helen M. Downey (New York, 1917).

24. See the letter quoted by Theodor Reik, *From Thirty Years with Freud* (New York and Toronto, 1940), p. 175.

25. We may also take note of the position opposite to Lawrence's, namely that art is valuable insofar as it approaches total control over the unconscious. See, for example, Franz Alexander's essay, "The Psychoanalyst Looks at Contemporary Art," *Art and Psychoanalysis,* ed. William Phillips (Cleveland and New York, 1963), pp. 346–365. Alexander defends his discomfort in the presence of modern art by equating abstraction with infantilism, and he wishfully predicts, "After the scientific mastery of the unconscious, its artistic mastery will follow" (p. 364). Here we may say that the therapeutic aim of psychoanalysis *has* been retained by the critic, and with a very banal result.

26. For a penetrating discussion of this prejudice and the whole matter of psychoanalytic terminology in criticism, see Lesser, *Fiction and the Unconscious,* pp. 294–308.

27. Leon Edel, "Notes on the Use of Psychological Tools in Literary Scholarship," *Literature and Psychology: Reprint of Leading Articles and Bibliographies from Volumes I and II* (September 1953), p. 8.

28. See Frederick Clarke Prescott, *The Poetic Mind* (New York, 1922), Otto Rank, *Art and Artist: Creative Urge and Personality Development* (New York, 1932), Hanns Sachs, *The Creative Unconscious: Studies in the Psychoanalysis of Art* (Cambridge, Mass., 1942, 1951), Roy P. Basler, *Sex, Symbolism and Psychology in Literature* (New Brunswick, N.J., 1948), Arthur Wormhoudt, *The Demon Lover: A Psychoanalytical Approach to Literature* (New York, 1949), Edmund Bergler, *The Writer and Psychoanalysis* (Garden City, N.Y., 1950), Daniel E. Schneider, *The Psychoanalyst and the Artist* (New York, 1950), and Philip Weissman, *Creativity in the Theater: A Psychoanalytic Study* (New York and London, 1965). For the effect of psychoanalysis on creative writers themselves, see Frederick J. Hoffman, *Freudianism and the Literary Mind* (Baton Rouge, La., 1945, 1957). Other psychological studies of literature may be located in Norman Kiell, *Psychoanalysis, Psychology, and Literature: A Bibliography* (Madison, Wis., 1963), and in the bibliographies and book reviews in the journal *Literature and Psychology.* See also Louis Fraiberg, *Psychoanalysis and American Literary Criticism* (Detroit, 1960).

29. See *On the Limits of Poetry: Selected Essays: 1928–1948* (New York, 1948), p. 53.

Chapter Two

1. Herbert Marcuse, *Eros and Civilization: A Philosophical Inquiry into Freud* (1955; rpt. New York, 1962), pp. 181, 216.
2. Herbert Marcuse, *One-Dimensional Man* (Boston, 1964), p. 231.
3. Norman O. Brown, *Life Against Death: The Psychoanalytical Meaning of History* (1959; rpt. New York, n.d.), p. 185. Hereafter cited parenthetically as *LD*.
4. Norman O. Brown, *Love's Body* (New York, 1966), p. 245. Hereafter cited parenthetically as *L's B*.
5. Norman O. Brown, "Apocalypse: The Place of Mystery in the Life of the Mind," *Harper's*, May 1961, pp. 46–49.
6. See John O. Wisdom, *The Unconscious Origin of Berkeley's Philosophy* (Oxford, 1953).
7. Sigmund Freud, "Fragment of an Analysis of a Case of Hysteria," *The Standard Edition of the Complete Psychological Works of Sigmund Freud*, ed. James Strachey *et al.*, 24 vols. (London, 1953–74), VII, 109.
8. Hayden V. White, "The Burden of History," *History and Theory*, 5 (1966), 111–134.
9. Philip Rieff, *The Triumph of the Therapeutic: Uses of Faith After Freud* (1966; rpt. New York and Evanston, 1968), p. 72.

Chapter Three

1. Marvin Mudrick, ed., *Conrad: A Collection of Critical Essays* (Englewood Cliffs, N.J., 1966), Introduction, p. 10.
2. F. R. Leavis, *The Great Tradition: A Study of the English Novel* (1948; rpt. Garden City, N.Y., 1954), p. 216.
3. But for Conrad the matter wasn't so easy. "Even writing to a friend—to a person one has heard, touched, drank with, quarrelled with—does not give me a sense of reality. All is illusion—the words written, the mind at which they are aimed, the truth they are intended to express, the hands that will hold the paper, the eyes that will glance at the lines. Every image floats vaguely in a sea of doubt—and the doubt itself is lost in an unexplored universe of incertitudes" (*Letters from Conrad, 1895–1924*, ed. Edward Garnett [London, 1928; rpt. Indianapolis and New York, 1962], p. 155). This is Leavis' "gallant simple sailor" whose genius was "a unique and happy union of seaman and writer" (Leavis, pp. 223, 229).

4. "Although qualified to enter nirvana, like the true Bodhisattva, Marlow remains in the world to work for the salvation of all people. In his stage of enlightenment he teaches what his descent into the imperfections of the human soul has taught him—egoless compassion. Cancelling out all personal desire and fear, he has made available to humanity the gift of complete renunciation. To every suffering, striving creature, trapped in the karmic processes (enslavement to matter), he offers the inexhaustible wisdom of selflessness" (William Bysshe Stein, "The Lotus Posture and *Heart of Darkness*," Norton Critical Edition of *Heart of Darkness*, ed. Robert Kimbrough [New York, 1963], p. 199).

5. Bernard C. Meyer, *Joseph Conrad: A Psychoanalytic Biography* (Princeton, N.J., 1967), p. 69.

6. For a fuller psychoanalytic discussion of this side of Conrad, see Norman N. Holland, "Style as Character: *The Secret Agent*," *Modern Fiction Studies*, 12 (Summer 1966), 221–231.

7. Albert Guerard, *Conrad the Novelist* (Cambridge, Mass., 1958), p. 257.

8. Jessie Conrad, *Conrad and His Circle* (New York, 1935), p. 27.

9. Leavis, for instance, feels cheered by a novel containing so many "upright, sensitive and humane individuals . . . —'we sailors,' the feeling is . . ." And he reminds us that Heyst, whatever his problems may have been, does make a "tragic pronouncement in favour of trust in life" (Leavis, p. 252)—shortly before committing suicide, but no matter.

10. Joseph Conrad, *Victory* (1915; rpt. New York, n.d.), pp. 372, 375, 377.

11. *Heart of Darkness* (note 4 above), pp. 65–66. Hereafter cited parenthetically as *HD*.

12. See, however, Richard F. Sterba's perceptive "Remarks on Joseph Conrad's *Heart of Darkness*," *Journal of the American Psychoanalytic Association*, 13 (July 1965), 570–583.

13. Both Kurtz and Korzeniowski—the names are alike—are intellectuals and versifiers; neither can be properly said to have a profession; both have dabbled in journalism and written pamphlets; both have messianic political ambitions and a mixture of refinement and demagoguery; both are accused of disrupting the orderly domination of a victimized territory; both die far from home, maintaining almost until the end a grandiloquent intention to return and prevail; both are remembered as prematurely withered and helpless, yet oppressive; both are famous for their arresting voices and their

ability to persuade; both seem addicted to self-pity; both refuse an offer of rescue; both leave literary remains; both profess a high-minded Christianity but have experimented with dissipation. The family of Kurtz's "Intended" objects to her engagement to him; so did Evelina Bobrowska's family object to her engagement to Apollo Korzeniowski. These parallels, all of which can be inferred by checking "Heart of Darkness" against Jocelyn Baines's biography of Conrad, receive further credence from Bernard Meyer's conclusion that "there was something of his father in every story [Conrad] had written" (Meyer, p. 285).

14. Zdzislaw Najder, *Conrad's Polish Background* (London, 1964), p. 11.

15. Of these allusions to childhood dependency one deserves special interest, not only because it has been a crux but because it epitomizes the privacy and anguished sincerity of the story's autobiographical reference. Marlow finds Kurtz attended by a remarkably boyish Russian, a "harlequin" with a peeling nose, who sits at Kurtz's feet and tries to think the best of him, as the well-bred, inwardly unforgiving Conrad must have done with his father in Russia. This figure of submission had formerly been rebellious against his father, an arch-priest; he "had run away from school, had gone to sea in a Russian ship; ran away again; served some time in English ships; was now reconciled with the arch-priest. He made a point of that" (*HD*, p. 54). Beyond question this is Conrad's own story, with the difference that Conrad finds reconciliation less feasible. But the image of the obedient harlequin has a still more precise origin in Conrad's memories. In the letter I have quoted as an epigraph he lamented his post-Congo depression and compared himself wistfully to the "Polichinelle"—or Pulcinello—of his childhood. This gentlemanly toy, he explained, had put up with all manner of tender abuse from its master. Despite such indignities as a broken nose and missing eye (the symbolism is obvious), and the licking off of its paint, the harlequin had "received my confidences with a sympathetic air. . . ." When Conrad, near the end of his tale of filial usurpation, tried to introduce an image of the reformed son, his latent cynicism hit upon this figure. To obey was to be a clown, a "polite little Pole" whose nose and eye were forfeit to the paternal avenger. See J. A. Gee and P. J. Sturm, eds., *Letters of Joseph Conrad to Marguerite Poradowska, 1890–1920* (New Haven, 1940), pp. 37–39.

16. Samuel Beckett, *Three Novels* (New York, 1965), p. 22.

Chapter Four

1. *Anatomy of Criticism: Four Essays* (Princeton, 1957), pp. 6–7; copyright © 1957 by Princeton University Press; reprinted by permission of Princeton University Press.
2. *Fearful Symmetry: A Study of William Blake* (Princeton, 1947).
3. Murray Krieger, "The Critical Legacy of Matthew Arnold; Or, The Strange Brotherhood of T. S. Eliot, I. A. Richards, and Northrop Frye," *Southern Review*, n.s. 5 (April 1969), 457–474.
4. René Wellek and Austin Warren, *Theory of Literature* (New York, 1949), pp. 75–88. For more up-to-date thinking, purportedly sympathetic, see Lee T. Lemon, *The Partial Critics* (New York, 1965), p. 94: "Neither proper psychological definition of *archetype* nor the relative soundness of Freud's and Jung's views of the content of the unconscious need concern the literary critic directly. The only significant fact is that elements do get into poetry which can best be explained by psychoanalytic theory." The likelihood that *some* theory is potentially useful exhausts the critic's curiosity; since he has no way of choosing between Freud and Jung, he calls them both "psychoanalytic" and drops the subject.
5. See Glover, *Freud or Jung* (London, 1950).
6. On these matters see Louis Kampf's essay-review of three books of literary history in *History and Theory*, 6 (1967), 72–88. See also R. J. Kaufmann, "On Knowing One's Place: A Humanistic Meditation," *Daedalus*, Summer 1969, pp. 699–713, and Allen Grossman, "Teaching Literature in a Discredited Civilization," *Massachusetts Review*, 10 (Summer 1969), 419–432.
7. Frye's "archetype" is not quite the same as Jung's; it is merely any "typical or recurring image" in literary tradition, and archetypal analysis is consequently "the study of conventions and genres" (Frye, p. 99).
8. It is supremely ironic that some frustrated students, deducing that any intellectual effort must be inimical to their neglected feelings, are now turning against "the mind" and discovering an ally in C. G. Jung—the Jung of numinosity, astrology, numerology, augury, alchemy, and the vulgarized Mysterious East.
9. This point is elaborated by Weston La Barre, "Family and Symbol," in George F. Wilbur and Warner Muensterberger, eds., *Psychoanalysis and Culture: Essays in Honor of Géza Róheim* (New York, 1967), pp. 156–167. La Barre's *The Human Animal* (Chicago and Lon-

don, 1960) and Alex Comfort's *The Nature of Human Nature* (New York, 1968) are helpful books for the layman.

10. Freud, "Five Lectures on Psycho-Analysis," *The Standard Edition of the Complete Psychological Works of Sigmund Freud,* ed. James Strachey *et al.* (hereafter abbreviated *S.E.*), 24 vols. (London, 1953–74), XI, 17.

11. Géza Róheim, *The Origin and Function of Culture* (New York, 1943), p. 100.

12. See especially Erik H. Erikson, *Young Man Luther: A Study in Psychoanalysis and History* (New York, 1958) and *Childhood and Society* (2nd ed.; New York, 1963); and Norman Cohn, *The Pursuit of the Millennium* (Fairlawn, N.J., 1957) and *Warrant for Genocide: The Myth of the Jewish World Conspiracy and the Protocols of the Elders of Zion* (London, 1967). The last of these books may remind us that more than a methodological quarrel stands between those who analyze the projective content of myths and those who celebrate them as awesome powers.

13. See *Psychoanalytic Explorations in Art* (London, 1953).

14. Quoted by Roy P. Basler, *Sex, Symbolism, and Psychology in Literature* (New Brunswick, N.J., 1948), p. 4.

15. Freud, "Repression," *S.E.*, XIV, 149.

16. Indeed, the theoretical difference between Chomsky's linguistic rationalism and Skinner's linguistic behaviorism is entirely parallel to the difference between a psychoanalytic view of literature and an antimotivational view that treats any given work as a product of "influences" derived in an unknown manner from previous works. Like innate linguistic capacity, innate psychic disposition must be posited to account for ascertainable regularities. This is not, of course, to say that Chomsky's refutation of Skinner justifies Freud. The point is that a relatively "constrained" notion of psychic uniformity may prove flexible where a relatively "free" notion breaks down. Skinner's shunning of hypotheses about linguistic capacity leaves him with no choice but to ascribe an incredible causative weight to the mere hearing of words and sentences; so, too, literary theorists who side-step the unconscious often end by deifying tradition and memory. See Noam Chomsky, "A Review of B. F. Skinner's *Verbal Behavior,*" in Jerry A. Fodor and Jerrold J. Katz, eds., *The Structure of Language: Readings in the Philosophy of Language* (Englewood Cliffs, N.J., 1964), pp. 547–579.

17. Introduction to Christina Stead, *The Man Who Loved Children* (New York, Chicago, San Francisco, 1965), p. xl.

18. Academic critics have made characteristic rhetorical use of Ernest

Jones's *Hamlet and Oedipus* (New York, 1949), taking its outdated scholarship and its literalism regarding fictional personages as reasons for dismissing the whole relevance of psychoanalysis to Shakespeare criticism. Meanwhile Jones's (and Freud's) central insight about the play has been confirmed and refined by other observers. See Simon O. Lesser, "Freud and *Hamlet* Again," *American Imago,* 12 (Fall 1955), 207–220, and the studies summarized in Norman N. Holland, *Psychoanalysis and Shakespeare* (New York, Toronto, London, 1966).

19. On this point see David Rapaport, *The Structure of Psychoanalytic Theory* (New York, 1960), Abraham Kaplan, *The Conduct of Inquiry: Methodology for Behavioral Science* (San Francisco, 1964), and Michael Sherwood, *The Logic of Explanation in Psychoanalysis* (New York and London, 1969).

20. See especially E. Pumpian-Mindlin, ed., *Psychoanalysis as Science: The Dixon Lectures on the Scientific Status of Psychoanalysis* (Stanford, 1952); Helen D. Sargent, "Intrapsychic Change: Methodological Problems in Psychotherapy Research," *Psychiatry,* 24 (1961), 93–108; and L. A. Gottschalk and A. H. Auerbach, eds., *Methods of Research in Psychotherapy* (New York, 1966).

21. See *The Sociological Imagination* (New York, 1959).

22. See, generally, Norman S. Greenfield and William C. Lewis, eds., *Psychoanalysis and Current Biological Thought* (Madison and Milwaukee, 1965). The essays by Herbert Weiner, John D. Benjamin, and Robert R. Holt are especially important.

23. New York, 1968.

24. Quoted by Hanna Segal, "A Psycho-Analytical Approach to Aesthetics," *International Journal of Psycho-Analysis,* 23 (1952), 206.

25. See *The Nation,* 192 (1961), 339–341. Holland's chief authority for eschewing value judgments is Northrop Frye, whom he admires for having "cleared the air of a great deal of obscurantist smog" (*Dynamics,* p. xvi; see also pp. 196–197).

26. That this is a consequence of Holland's model and not a personal limitation is apparent from his excellent essay, "H.D. and the 'Blameless Physician,' " *Contemporary Literature,* 10 (Autumn 1969), 474–506.

27. Alfred North Whitehead, *The Aims of Education* (New York, 1929), p. 139.

28. For a comparable argument from the standpoint of perception psychology, see Morse Peckham, *Man's Rage for Chaos: Biology, Behavior, and the Arts* (Philadelphia, 1965).

29. Certain Freudian romantics, of whom the best known is Norman

O. Brown, regard history itself as a gigantic tussle between the psychic forces posited by psychoanalysis. No such "psychologism" is being asserted here. A position like Brown's lends support to the accusation that psychoanalysis wants to replace other styles of observation by collapsing them into a general pathology. This is psychic determinism with a vengeance, but it is not psychoanalysis. Since my own essay may be subject to misunderstanding on this score, let me emphasize that psychoanalytic discourse properly seeks to show how individuals and groups *respond to* a totality of inner and outer conditions, and that for this task an awareness of nonpsychological forces is indispensable. (The point was made most clearly by Otto Fenichel, "The Drive to Amass Wealth," in his *Collected Papers,* Second Series [New York, 1954], pp. 89–108.) As applied to literature, this position not only welcomes but insists upon knowledge of every operative factor, including genre, convention, rhetorical devices, philosophical intent, audience, class, and personal background. What psychoanalysis disputes is not the usefulness of such information, but the equation of it with literary experience.

30. *Beyond Good and Evil,* in *The Complete Works of Friedrich Nietzsche,* ed. Oscar Levy, 18 vols. (New York, 1964), XII, 85.

Chapter Five

1. See Halle, "The Student Drive to Destruction," *New Republic,* October 19, 1968; Kennan, *Democracy and the Student Left* (Boston and Toronto, 1968); Barzun, *The American University: How It Runs, Where It Is Going* (New York, Evanston, and London, 1968); Howe, "The New York Intellectuals: A Chronicle and a Critique," *Commentary,* October 1968; Trilling, "On the Steps of Low Library: Liberalism and the Revolution of the Young," *Commentary,* November 1968; and Schlesinger, *Violence: America in the Sixties* (New York, 1968).

2. C. Wright Mills, *The Marxists* (New York, 1963), p. 29.

3. Lewis S. Feuer, *The Conflict of Generations: The Character and Significance of Student Movements* (New York and London, 1969).

4. Eveoleen N. Rexford, "Children, Child Psychiatry, and Our Brave New World," *Archives of General Psychiatry,* 20 (January 1969), 25–37.

5. William M. Birenbaum, *Overlive: Power, Poverty, and the University* (New York, 1969); Immanuel Wallerstein, *University in Turmoil: The Politics of Change* (New York, 1969).

6. See Glazer's "The New Left and Its Limits," *Commentary*, June 1968, pp. 31–39, and " 'Student Power' in Berkeley," *The Public Interest*, Fall 1968, pp. 3–21.
7. Hare is quoted extensively by John H. Bunzel, "Black Studies at San Francisco State," *The Public Interest*, Fall 1968, pp. 22–38.
8. Eldridge Cleaver, *Soul on Ice* (New York, 1968), p. 77.

Chapter Six

1. Martin Nicolaus, "The Professional Organization of Sociology: A View from Below," *Antioch Review*, 24 (Fall 1969), 381.
2. See David Horowitz, "Sinews of Empire," *Ramparts*, October 1969, p. 42, and Harry Magdoff, *The Age of Imperialism* (New York, 1969).
3. See Rostow, *The United States in the World Arena: An Essay in Recent History* (New York, 1960), and *The Stages of Economic Growth: A Non-Communist Manifesto* (Cambridge, Eng., 1961); and Galbraith, *The New Industrial State* (Boston, 1967). Whether Galbraith is truly naïve in this omission and in some of his assertions, such as that the corporations are now run by their middle-level bureaucrats and engineers and are no longer interested in profit, is hard to ascertain; what is striking is that his book is taken seriously by intelligent liberals.
4. See Seymour Melman, *Our Depleted Society* (New York, 1965). Ironically, even the war contractors have suffered; see George E. Berkeley, "The Myth of War Profiteering," *New Republic*, December 20, 1969, pp. 15–18.
5. The alleged unities are often religious, even in some instances where the writer was a notorious scoffer. Such misperception might be traced not only to the critic's personal background, which may have been quite secular, but also to our society's reduction of all problems to questions of personal morality and to its interest in higher rationales for earthly injustice. The heyday of crypto-religious criticism was, naturally enough, the Eisenhower period.

Chapter Seven

1. Andrew Kopkind, "The Greening of America: Beyond the Valley of the Heads," *Ramparts*, March 1971, p. 52.
2. I am excluding some elements often considered to be part of the New Left, chiefly the ethnic minorities and women who have sought power on their own behalf. The Movement as I construe it

has shared tactics with these groups but has differed from them in its psychology and goals.

3. Peter Marin, "The Open Truth and Fiery Vehemence of Youth: A Sort of Soliloquy," in Mitchell Goodman, ed., *The Movement Toward a New America: The Beginnings of a Long Revolution* (Philadelphia and New York, 1970), p. 9.

4. David Horowitz, "Revolutionary Karma vs. Revolutionary Politics," *Ramparts*, March 1971, p. 29.

5. Susan Sontag, "Some Thoughts on the Right Way (for us) to Love the Cuban Revolution," *Ramparts*, April 1969, p. 10.

6. Both Marcuse and Reich are praised for their very extravagance in Paul A. Robinson, *The Freudian Left: Wilhelm Reich, Geza Roheim, Herbert Marcuse* (New York, Evanston, and London, 1969). "All three thinkers," says Robinson appreciatively, "are eminently injudicious; they harbor only contempt for the pluralistic tolerance of the liberal imagination" (p. 6). Whether any of them made plausible statements about the world is of only fleeting concern to Robinson. For an illuminating discussion of Laing's politics see David Martin, "R. D. Laing: Psychiatry and Apocalypse," *Dissent*, June 1971, pp. 235–251.

7. *The Making of a Counter Culture: Reflections on the Technocratic Society and Its Youthful Opposition* (Garden City, N.Y., 1969), p. 240. Roszak's appeal is made not only to Marcuse, Brown, and Watts, but to "oracles, dervishes, yogis, sibyls, prophets, druids, etc.—the whole heritage of mystagoguery toward which the beat-hip wing of our counter culture now gravitates" (p. 247).

8. Sontag, to her credit, draws attention to the differences between the Cuban revolutionary outlook and the counter culture's. Her essay tactfully advises young leftists to avoid superimposing one situation on the other—which is exactly what they do.

9. Marcuse's mechanistic application of Hegel's Absolutism to history is discussed by Alasdair MacIntyre, *Herbert Marcuse: An Exposition and a Polemic* (New York, 1970), pp. 21–41.

10. *Literature and Revolution*, tr. Rose Strunsky (Ann Arbor, 1960), p. 191.

11. Donald Lazere, "Down With Culture?", *Village Voice*, September 11, 1969, p. 28.

12. Louis Kampf, "Notes Toward a Radical Culture," *The New Left: A Collection of Essays*, ed. Priscilla Long (Boston, 1969), p. 422.

13. An instructive example of the Movement's attitude toward radical scholarship is a review in *Ramparts* of Alvin W. Gouldner's *The*

Coming Crisis of Western Sociology, a book which, in reducing all Establishment sociology to Talcott Parsons, ought to have satiated anyone's taste for antipluralism. The reviewer praised Gouldner's book for demolishing sociology but added resentfully that it was, after all, only a presentation of ideas and not the fruit of revolutionary praxis in the streets. At a certain point Movement *machismo* had to be invoked and turned against the left-wing academic who seemed to take sociology too seriously as an autonomous discipline. Debate was thus shifted from the arena of rival ideas to that of rival postures, with the young reviewer and his brothers emerging as the true militants.

14. John McDermott, *The Nation,* March 10, 1969, pp. 296–301.
15. Cf. Jackie Di Salvo, "This Murder: New Criticism and Scholarship," *NUC-MLC Newsletter,* 1, no. 3 (n.d.), 11: "The poet, according to William Blake, is imprisoned like the rest of us but he serves us by singing about that cage. Having heard his song we must turn our energies to the bastille itself."
16. Katherine Ellis, "The Function of Northrop Frye at the Present Time," *College English,* 31 (March 1970), 544.
17. Louis Kampf, "The Trouble with Literature . . . ," *Change,* May–June 1970, p. 30.
18. In a lecture, "The Arts," delivered at the New School in October 1970, Marcuse extended his equation of deviance and revolution to the literary realm. It is true, he said, that the bourgeois classics superficially encourage a resigned affirmation, but they are negative at the core. As an example he mentioned the theme of the noble prostitute in Balzac. Nothing could better epitomize bourgeois sentimentalism than that theme, but by Marcuse's neo-Hegelian scorekeeping it constituted an item of negation and hence a point for the revolution. The unstated, but unmistakable, purpose of his lecture was to dissociate himself from the New Left's windmill-tilting campaign against literature—without, however, challenging the New Left's habit of doing a security check on all authors dead and alive. Marcuse simply proposed that the standards be relaxed to allow an imprimatur for his favorite texts.
19. Bruce Franklin, "The Teaching of Literature in the Highest Academies of the Empire," *College English,* 31 (March 1970), 556. Franklin adds that the professors' strategy—to assign tepidly quietistic works and reinforce their oppressive influence by diverting conscious attention to their formal properties—failed to pacify the politically awakened students:

So it was necessary to find less subtle vehicles of counter-revolutionary ideology. Alexander Pope and the metaphysical poets, Nathaniel Hawthorne and the Romantics, could hardly lure many students away from the contradictions of their own society or lead them into a reactionary view of them. Stronger medicine was needed, outright reactionary tracts written by contemporaries, works like *Lord of the Flies* and *Animal Farm,* which come right out and say in terms that everyone can understand: Man is nothing but a pig. *[p. 556]*

20. See also Barbara Bailey Kessel, "Free, Classless, and Urbane?", *College English,* 31 (March 1970), 531–540.
21. Roberta Salper, "Literature and Revolution in Cuba," *Monthly Review,* 22 (October 1970), 15–30.
22. Before telling us more about Socialist Realism Professor Salper might want to look at Edward J. Brown, *The Proletarian Episode in Russian Literature 1928–1932* (New York, 1953); Herman Ermolaev, *Soviet Literary Theories 1917–1934: The Genesis of Socialist Realism* (Berkeley and Los Angeles, 1963); and for the human interest angle, Nadezhda Mandelstam, *Hope Against Hope: A Memoir* (New York, 1970).
23. Louis Kampf, "The Humanities and Inhumanities," *The Nation,* September 30, 1968; the quotation, lacking italics, is on p. 312.
24. Louis Kampf, "The Scandal of Literary Scholarship," *Harper's,* December 1967, p. 89.
25. Jean-Paul Sartre, *What is Literature?,* tr. Bernard Frechtman (New York, 1965), p. 45.

Chapter Eight

1. Program, *Symposium on Orgone Energy and Bio-energetics* (Berkeley: KPFA, 1974), p. 2. Farrar, Straus and Giroux and its Noonday imprint have now republished Reich's *The Cancer Biopathy, Character Analysis, Ether, God and Devil and Cosmic Superimposition, The Function of the Orgasm, The Invasion of Compulsory Sex-Morality, Listen, Little Man!, The Mass Psychology of Fascism, The Murder of Christ, Reich Speaks of Freud, Selected Writings,* and *The Sexual Revolution.* Writings from Reich's period as an active leftist have been collected in *Sex-Pol: Essays, 1929–1934,* ed. Lee Baxandall (New York, 1972). A leading disciple, Ola Raknes, has surveyed Reich's career in *Wilhelm Reich and Orgonomy* (1970; rpt. Baltimore, 1971). Reich is viewed skeptically by Philip Rieff, *The Triumph of the Therapeutic: Uses of Faith After Freud* (1966; rpt. New York and Evanston, 1968)

and by Charles Rycroft, *Wilhelm Reich* (New York, 1971); this is the book in the "Modern Masters" series. His importance to the cultural left has been explored by Paul A. Robinson, *The Freudian Left: Wilhelm Reich, Geza Roheim, Herbert Marcuse* (1969; rpt. New York, n.d.) and by Richard King, *The Party of Eros: Radical Social Thought and the Realm of Freedom* (Chapel Hill, N.C., 1972). In *Orgone, Reich and Eros: Wilhelm Reich's Theory of Life Energy* (New York, 1973) W. Edward Mann presents Reich as one of the foremost modern geniuses, though an eccentric and intemperate one. Eustace Chesser gives Reich high marks as a therapeutic innovator in *Salvation Through Sex: The Life and Work of Wilhelm Reich* (New York, 1973). Reich's practical political activism is emphasized by Michel Cattier, *The Life and Work of Wilhelm Reich*, tr. Ghislaine Boulanger (1971; rpt. New York, 1973). His world view is enthusiastically defended by Elsworth Baker, *Man in the Trap* (New York, 1967), Orson Bean, *Me and the Orgone: The True Story of One Man's Sexual Awakening* (1971; rpt. Greenwich, Conn., 1972), and James Wyckoff, *Wilhelm Reich: Life Force Explorer* (Greenwich, Conn., 1973). His reputation as a martyr is enhanced by Jerome Greenfield, *Wilhelm Reich versus the USA* (New York, 1974). And the most comprehensive discussion of Reich's scientific claims is David Boadella, *Wilhelm Reich: The Evolution of his Work* (Chicago, 1973).

2. Paul Goodman, *Drawing the Line* (1946; rpt. New York, 1962), p. 4.

3. Norman Mailer, "The White Negro: Superficial Reflections on the Hipster," *Advertisements for Myself* (1959; rpt. New York, 1966), p. 313.

4. Introduction to Isaac Rosenfeld, *An Age of Enormity: Life and Writing in the Forties and Fifties* (Cleveland and New York, 1962), p. 34.

5. See Kate Millett, *Sexual Politics* (1971; rpt. New York, 1973), and Juliet Mitchell, *Psychoanalysis and Feminism* (New York, 1974).

6. A staggeringly large, though incomplete, list of Reich's purported discoveries is provided by the editors of his *Selected Writings: An Introduction to Orgonomy* (New York, 1973), pp. xvii–xviii. In further parenthetical references this volume will be designated *SW*.

7. Raknes, *Wilhelm Reich and Orgonomy* (note 1 above), p. 67.

8. "What characterizes the empirical method," as Karl R. Popper remarks, "is its manner of exposing to falsification, in every conceivable way, the system to be tested. Its aim is not to save the lives of untenable systems but . . . to select the one which is by comparison the fittest, by exposing them all to the fiercest struggle for survival" (*The Logic of Scientific Discovery* [New York, 1959], p. 42).

9. Boadella, *Wilhelm Reich* (note 1), p. 177.

10. It follows that a critic who first agrees and then disagrees with Reich's escalating claims must have suffered an orgastic setback. Thus Freud, in Reich's view, was "just a simple animal" (this is a compliment) during their early acquaintance, but later, when their ideas diverged, he must have been "simply love-starved"—the delayed effect, apparently, of "the severe inhibition imposed by a Jewish family and a Jewish bride upon his very alive and emotionally longing bio-system" (*Reich Speaks of Freud: Wilhelm Reich Discusses His Work and His Relationship with Sigmund Freud*, ed. Mary Higgins and Chester M. Raphael [1967; rpt. New York, 1972], pp. 37, 58n., 130). Never for a moment does Reich consider that Freud may have rejected some of his ideas on their merits. The ideas are assumed to be patently correct but also threatening to every existing order. Because "he was very much dissatisfied genitally" (p. 20), Freud lacked the courage to reveal the truth, leaving Reich "to carry the heavy burden of psychoanalysis alone" (p. 215).

11. See Raknes, p. 94, and Reich, *SW*, pp. 209–210.

12. Michael Polanyi, *Personal Knowledge: Towards a Post-Critical Philosophy* (1958; rpt. New York and Evanston, 1964), p. 230.

13. In Karl Mannheim's words, "Life in terms of an inner balance which must be ever won anew is the essentially novel element which modern man . . . must elaborate for himself if he is to live on the basis of the rationality of the Enlightenment" (*Ideology and Utopia: An Introduction to the Sociology of Knowledge*, tr. Louis Wirth and Edward Shils [1936; rpt. New York, n.d.], p. 35).

14. Orson Bean, *Me and the Orgone* (note 1 above), pp. 26, 90, 39, 40, 63, 90, 159.

15. Quoted by Rycroft, *Wilhelm Reich* (note 1 above), pp. 69, 70.

16. Thus, for example, he praises the lucidity of a schizophrenic patient bedevilled by "forces": "What deep thought, and how close to the truth! I assure the reader that at that time she knew nothing of the orgone phenomena and that I had not told her anything about them" (*Character Analysis*, 3rd ed. [1933, 1945; rpt. New York, 1972], p. 421).

17. R. D. Laing, *The Politics of Experience* (1967; rpt. New York, 1968), pp. 144–145.

18. See *The Murder of Christ: The Emotional Plague of Mankind* (1953; rpt. New York, 1971).

19. In Mailer's case the therapeutic use of paranoid-style reasoning is especially conspicuous. He feels relieved when he contrives to identify with "two strong eighteen-year-old hoodlums, let us say,

[who] beat in the brains of a candy-store keeper." As Mailer reassures us, "one murders not only a weak fifty-year-old man but an institution as well . . . The hoodlum is therefore daring the unknown . . ." (pp. 320–321).

20. "If two orgonotic systems with different charges are connected, the more heavily laden system will draw energy from the weaker system, until the weaker system can give off no more . . ." (Raknes, pp. 38–39).

21. "I have to save my clean thoughts," Reich told Kurt Eissler in 1952. "I have to maintain a cleanliness, a purity. Freud didn't succeed in that, and you can see it in his face" (*RSF*, p. 35). Addressing his fellow mortals, he fumed: "I have no filthy phantasy like you, Little Man" (*Listen, Little Man!* [New York, 1948], p. 112). From his third ex-wife we learn that he especially loathed and avoided homosexuals (see, generally, Ilse Ollendorf Reich, *Wilhelm Reich: A Personal Biography* [1967; rpt. New York, 1970]). And Reich thought of his late cosmic discoveries as placing him beyond the reach of an ungrateful mankind. "And since you are dangerous to life," he told us in the 1940's, "since in your proximity one cannot stick to the truth without being stabbed in the back and without having dirt thrown into one's face, I have separated myself. . . . For I have important things to do. *I have discovered the living*, Little Man. Now I no longer confuse you with the living which I felt in myself and sought in you" (*Listen, Little Man!*, p. 105; italics in original).

22. Reich looked forward to a future dispensation in which, to ensure peace of mind, "any kind of literature which creates sexual anxiety must be prohibited"; "Every mass organization will have to have sexologically well-trained functionaries who have no other job than that of observing the development of the organization with regard to sexuality . . . and to tackle the difficulties in conjunction with a central sexological agency"; and "The whole population must have the secure understanding that the government does everything possible to secure sexual happiness" (*The Sexual Revolution: Toward a Self-Governing Character Structure*, tr. Theodore P. Wolfe [1945, 1969; rpt. New York, 1971], pp. 262, 264).

Chapter Nine

1. Michael West, "Scatology and Eschatology: The Heroic Dimensions of Thoreau's Wordplay," *PMLA*, 89 (October 1974), 1045–1061.

2. Norman N. Holland, *The Dynamics of Literary Response* (New York, 1968), p. 27.

3. *Dynamics*, p. 27. This is the alleged "heart" of the Wife of Bath's Tale.

4. For representative works, see Anna Freud, *The Ego and the Mechanisms of Defense*, rev. ed. (New York, 1966); Heinz Hartmann, *Ego Psychology and the Problem of Adaptation* (New York, 1958); Heinz Hartmann, Ernst Kris, and Rudolph Loewenstein, "Comments on the Formation of Psychic Structure," *The Psychoanalytic Study of the Child*, 2 (1946), 11–37; Ernst Kris, *Psychoanalytic Explorations in Art* (London, 1953); Robert Waelder, "The Principle of Multiple Function," *Psychoanalytic Quarterly*, 5 (1936), 45–62; David Rapaport, *The Structure of Psychoanalytic Theory* (New York, 1960); and Erik H. Erikson, *Childhood and Society*, 2nd ed. (New York, 1963).

5. The preceding paragraphs needn't be taken as a blanket rejection of ego psychology; they apply more narrowly to efforts to qualify, without fundamentally reexamining, Freud's epigenetic determinism. Some ego psychologists have been conducting just such a drastic review. See, for example, the recent articles of Roy Schafer, of which a fair example is "The Idea of Resistance," *International Journal of Psycho-Analysis*, 54 (1973), 259–285. Interestingly, however, psychoanalysis in Schafer's hands is not so much a general theory of personality formation as it is a gloss on the unfolding dialogue between analyst and patient—a fascinating gloss, but one whose transposability to other settings is greatly diminished. When the deterministic assumptions lying behind Freudian terminology are exposed and found to be unsupportable on the basis of clinical evidence, psychoanalysis loses most of its explanatory promise. This point does not seem to be fully appreciated in the Hartmann-Rapaport mainstream of ego psychology.

6. See, for example, W. R. D. Fairbairn, *An Object-Relations Theory of the Personality* (New York, 1954); Edith Jacobson, *The Self and the Object World* (New York, 1964); and D. W. Winnicott, *Playing and Reality* (London, 1971).

7. An ambitious book by Holland entitled *Five Readers Reading* is to be published soon. Meanwhile we have, among other items, *Poems in Persons: An Introduction to the Psychoanalysis of Literature* (New York, 1973) and a manifesto entitled "A Letter to Leonard," *Hartford Studies in Literature*, 5 (1973), 9–30. It should be understood that Holland's own view of his progress after the *Dynamics* bears no resemblance to the account given below. If I insist on emphasizing the struggle against reductionism and insularity, rather than (as

Holland would have it) the completion of a solid theoretical edifice, it is because I credit Holland with an unacknowledged sensitivity to the issues that were highlighted by the reception of his earlier work.

8. For the theory of identity themes, see Heinz Lichtenstein, "Identity and Sexuality: A Study of Their Interrelationship in Man," *Journal of the American Psychoanalytic Association*, 9 (1961), 179–260. Lichtenstein's notion strikingly illustrates the specious gain in flexibility sometimes held out by revisions of Freud. The idea of the identity theme, to be sure, credits the subject with more activity and responsibility in apprehending the world than does the Freudian idea of fixation to trauma. Yet it also pegs each writer's formula of conflict management when he is scarcely ambulatory and encourages the analyst to find that formula exemplified in every one of his expressions. The oral, anal, urethral, and phallic fantasies that Holland formerly stressed look by comparison like manifestations of the freedom of the will; for now we get, not one fantasy for *Volpone* and another for *The Alchemist*, but one identity theme for Jonson running through all his doomed efforts to achieve variety.

9. Nor, with "one unique exception" (*Poems in Persons*, p. 6), can we know authors' minds other than "tautologically," through study of the very works that invite our projections. The exception is H. D., about whom Holland had already written an essay before arriving at his current pyrrhonism. Because H. D. left us a memoir of her analysis with Freud, she becomes the one accessible mind among world authors.

10. Where the readers do agree, a further doubt arises as to whether Holland's subjects may not be excessively influenced by his own expectations. Here are some excerpts from three responses to Frost's "Once by the Pacific":

> Sarah: "In an analysis or interpretation of the poem I think I could do a pretty good job demonstrating the primal scene imagery of the poem."
> Seymour: "This poem shrieks to me, 'Primal scene.' "
> Sherwood: "Frost's poem has the same kind of [primal scene] fantasy material, but it's not as powerful as 'Dover Beach' " ("A Letter to Leonard," pp. 11, 16, 24).

These appear to be, not three readers reading, but three students doing what comes naturally in their predicament, i.e., humoring the teacher.

11. See Paul Ricoeur, *Freud and Philosophy*, tr. Denis Savage (New Haven and London, 1970).

12. See Karl Popper, *The Logic of Scientific Discovery* (London, 1959) and *The Open Society and Its Enemies*, 5th ed., Vol. 2 (1966, rpt. Princeton, 1971), esp. pp. 215–217.

13. Murray M. Schwartz, "The Space of Psychological Criticism," *Hartford Studies in Literature*, 5 (1973), xiv.

14. Harold Bloom, *The Anxiety of Influence: A Theory of Poetry* (New York, 1973).

INDEX

Index